To— A Very Special Friend
Carol Kidney
May God Bless You
Thru all the Days of
your life with His
Love, Joy and Protection
        With Love,
        Vada Caldwell
        May 1, 2017

Inspirational Memories and Poems

By Vada

Published by Innovo Publishing LLC
www.innovopublishing.com
1-888-546-2111

Providing Full-Service Publishing Services for
Christian Authors, Artists & Organizations: Hardbacks, Paperbacks,
eBooks, Audiobooks, Music & Film

ISBN: 978-1-61314-367-4

Cover Design & Interior Layout: Innovo Publishing LLC

Printed in the United States of America
U.S. Printing History
First Edition: January 2017

The Author

Poetry has been a part of my life since I was a child. My husband, Tommy always encouraged me to write. It has always been my desire to publish my writings. Recently my children and friends have urged me to follow my dream. So at the age of eighty-eight years I am stepping out in faith.

I have written poems over the years to my family and friends for birthday greetings and other special occasions. My poems are about love of family, the blessings of life, and about God and His creation. I am thankful for the talent God has given me, and the joy it brings to my life and the life of others.

On May 21, 1928 in Roger Springs, Tennessee, the youngest of four children, Vada Manelle Henson was born to L. D. Henson and Annie Wilma Yopp Henson.

On June 15, 1946 Vada married Thomas H. Caldwell, Jr. at Parkway Methodist Church in Memphis, Tennessee. We were blessed with three children; Cynthia Anne, Thomas H., III and Mary Catherine. Then along came eight grandchildren, twenty-four great grandchildren and four great-great grandchildren.

These precious children blessed our lives daily. My husband and I walked hand in hand and heart to heart, praising God for His goodness until his death in 2009.

Dear God, help me always to do Thy Will. Give me your strength, wisdom and knowledge so I might write this book to give honor and glory to your name.

Vada Henson Caldwell

Vada Henson 1944

Dedication

I dedicate this book to my Lord and Savior Jesus Christ, to my loved ones who have gone on before me, my mother and father, two brothers; Vernon and Roy, one sister Maggie Ruth Stephenson and my beautiful daughter-in-law Nancy Caldwell who lost her fight with cancer in 2007.

To my beloved husband who went to be with the Lord in 2009, my precious daughter Mary Catherine Caldwell Farr who left this world in 2012 and my angel granddaughter Lorrie Beth Caldwell Leach who God called home in 2014.

Each one was a very special part of my life, heart and soul, a true blessing from God.

Dear Friends,

With a joyful heart, I am thankful for your presence in my life. I am very happy you are reading my book. I hope with all my heart you will receive blessings and peace as you read.

Realizing there is a peace that can only be found in God's presence and that God's presence is found in prayer, I pray for you and yours. I pray each of you will have a full and blessed life all day every day in God's presence.

With God's Love and Mine,

Vada Henson Caldwell

September, 2016

Dreams

That which is only a dream
Shall come true some day
And life's beautiful stream
Come to life if we pray.

Our prayer shall be answered
If we pray in earnest
None shall go unanswered
Where there is a golden harvest.

If you believe in God and man.
Peace and happiness will come to you
And all others over the land
So to God and man always be true.

Written by Vada Henson - 1944

Heartache

The turmoil of all men's souls
Are worse than ever before
Has a depth that has never been told
In all the days of yore.

As told in the world of today
With pain and heartache for everyone
Not roses but thorns most of the way
And not one perfect person under the sun.

A well of loneliness all over the land
For someone very dear to you
Has taken your heart in hand
Only to prove untrue.

Someone you think to be the highest
Twists your heart with pain
And try to comfort with words of cheer
But all is in vain.

Written by Vada Henson - 1944

You

How happy we could be
If only you could see
That together we belong
Darling I can't be wrong.

Since you have gone
I am all alone
Please come home to me
And together we will be.

We'll build a little cottage by the sea
Someday we may be three
If only you could see
How happy we would be.

We'll grow so old together
And talk about the weather
Together we belong
Darling I can't be wrong.

Written by Vada Henson - April 24, 1945

My Prayer

Each night I say my little prayer,
For the one I shall always love;
And for all the boys over there,
And someday my prayer will be answered by God above.

I pray that the world will soon be free,
A world of love and trust;
My loved one will come back to me,
And we shall raise our children in a clean world
free of lust.

Written by:
Vada Henson - 1945

Unfinished and Unnamed

The wonderful knowledge of Love
Is the main beauty of life.
And like beautiful wings of a dove
Away will fly our strife.

Written in 1945 by Vada Henson

To You

Please always be mine
And give me your heart
Our love will be divine
And we shall never part.

You are the one for me,
Forever and ever;
With each other we will be
For we belong together.

To you I will be true,
For my heart belongs to you;
Come fly away with me
And yours I will ever be.

Written by:

Vada Henson

April 24, 1945

Vada Henson Caldwell
Thomas H. Caldwell, Jr.
Wedding Day June 15, 1946,
Parkway Methodist Church

To My Husband

The only gift I have for thee,
Is all the love in my heart.
I promise together we shall always be,
And we will never ever part.

Anything I ever do or say
My darling, I hope and pray
That you can always see
My heart belongs to thee.

You mean the world to me
And there is nothing I would not do
To prove to you, I'll always be
Right here beside you.

Written by:

Your loving wife, Vada

December, 1946

Thomas Herbert Caldwell, Jr.

My husband, my love and my life.
When I look into your eyes of blue
I know our love is pure and true.

And oh how blessed I am to be your wife!

By Vada

My Question - His Answer

I asked, Do you love me?
Tell me, please tell.
He replied, of course I do
My sweet Vada Manelle
And you know it very well!!!

VHC

You Are Mine

You are my child. I listen with love
As I watch from Heaven above.
At my feet you must humbly kneel
As you come to me in prayer
All your trouble and sorrow I will heal.

As thoughts come into your heart
Bow your head and let the words flow
Speak them in silence or aloud,
While you walk the path on earth below
Live your life in a way to make me proud.
Hold close to me and my word, never depart.

I hold you in my hand, you are mine.
For me, always let your light shine.
I know your desire, I know your need
I am here at your side
Have faith as the tiny mustard seed
And with me always abide.

From the heart of

Vada Henson Caldwell

Waiting

Three little noses pressed flat against the window pane
Searching each car that passed their way
But woe, woe, Grandma and Granddaddy never came.
Looking and watching till it was no longer day.

For shame, for shame
Grandma and Granddaddy never came
They jumped every time the telephone rang
But they listened and looked in vain.
They all spent the day
Wishing company would arrive
Out of expected happiness, big and gay
Only disappointment and sorrow was derived.

Two little girls and one little boy
Knew Grandma and Granddaddy were in town
And looked forward to their visit with joy,
But the day and night went by without a sound.

While getting ready for bed
One little boy said,
Well, I believe they forgot
Two little girls said, they sure better not.

Two little girls and one little boy
Were tucked away for the night
Mother sat down without much joy
No company today, what a sorrowful plight.

Do you think they love us or not?
Was the question we silently pondered.
Surely they do and care a whole lot.
They both were terribly missed
By children and mother as well.

Written by: Vada Caldwell – 1958

New Year's Day 1965

It's time again for New Year's Resolutions. I don't really like to make resolutions for a whole year. I much prefer to make them for just one day at a time. Like the old hymn which goes something like this:

"I don't worry about tomorrow, I just live from day to day." I like this philosophy. It seems to me it is less trying to just take it one day at a time or even one hour.

God broke our years into hours and days
So hour by hour and day by day
We may be able all the while
To be ever so strong.

Should the weight of all our troubles of this life
Meet us face to face in one place
I fear we would find it oh so hard to finish the race.
And find it hard to manage our strife.

We could not go
Our feet would stop; and so
God lays a little on us every day
And never, never on all the way.

If our burdens cut so deep
And our pathway be so steep
We still can go on by God's power
If only we bear the burden
Hour by Hour.

Vada Caldwell

Religion

In Webster's Dictionary we find a definition of religion. "An awareness or conviction of the existence of a supreme being arousing reverence, love, gratitude and the will to obey". Certainly all of us individually feel the need for religion and believe in God and worship Him. Our fore-fathers founded this blessed country on a belief in God and the unalienable rights of the individual to life, liberty and the pursuit of happiness.

There is more to Webster's definition, "devotion, or fidelity, and the will to serve. Can we find a parallel here to the philosophy of our individual lives? That is – common bond group joined together and devoted to the idea of providing the individual members of our church with spiritual enrichment, faithful to the principle of service to each other and our less fortunate fellowman at the same time. If this is a true picture of our philosophy and we follow it, we must be imbued with the sincere desire to help each other in every way possible.

Mr. Edward Filene said, "True religion is not in professing it, but rather in living it". Was this benevolent gentleman including the philosophy on which the Church was founded? I believe he was. Are you and I doing our part to further the spiritual life of our fellow men? What have we done lately? What are we planning to do in the future? Are we expecting someone else to do it? Don't wait – do it now. The Church needs you – You need the Church.

Written and spoken for a Sunday School lesson in 1966.

Mrs. Thomas H. Caldwell, Jr. (Vada)

Picture of Christ

Hanging in my living room is a picture of Christ in a frame of gold filigree, faintly illuminated by a tiny fluorescent light.

The simplicity of the coloring in the painting enhances its beauty. The only color noticeable is the deep purple of the flowing robe which Christ wears.

The figure of Christ is emphasized by one single ray of sunshine. Visible at first glance is the barren land and small bushes of thorns at the base of the rock where Christ kneels.

The expression on his face captures your heart as you feel the desolate loneliness of this great Savior of men as He prays alone in the Garden of Gethsemane.

Written by Vada Caldwell

1967

Moment by Moment, Day by Day

God in His wisdom broke our years into days and hours,
That we might live every day, one at a time
So we might be able to see
By living every hour, one at a time
Just how beautiful life can be.

Worry not about tomorrow and what is in store
Treasure the day and its riches, one day at a time
Think not about how many minutes, hours and days more
Are yours for the living and cherishing so fine.

Begin each day with God as your guide
And you will find at the end of that day
He is still there by your side
And listening with open arms as you pray.

So don't complicate your life
with uncertainty and strife
Ask God to help you see the way
To live each day for that day.

Forget all sorrows and pain
Treasure your youth and happiness sublime
For in the future you have everything to gain
By just living one day at a time.

Written by: Mrs. Vada Caldwell
August 1967

Savior Divine

Dear Savior, help me every day
To love more dearly as I pray;
I would walk daily by Thy side
And trust in Thee whate're betide.

Help me to live so near to Thee
Thy likeness may be seen in me;
Make me so gentle, kind and true
That I will do as Thou wouldst do.

To win some precious souls for Thee,
My errand here on earth would be;
And every day till Thou shalt come
To do some good, to help someone.

Written by:

Vada Henson Caldwell

August 26, 1967

And whatsoever ye do in word or deed, do all in the name of the Lord
Jesus, giving thanks to God and the Father by Him. (Col. 3:17)

My Three Children – Cindy, Tommy & Cathy Caldwell
at different stages of their life

Tommy, Cathy & Cindy

Cindy, Tommy & Cathy

Cathy, Tommy & Cindy

Tommy, Cindy & Cathy

Long Ago

In days of long ago
To each other we pledged our love
The days seemed to be so slow
And we wished our life away.

We shared our life day by day
Many the times of joy along the way
My love for you continued to grow
In our days of long ago.

If only we could have known
The harvest our future would hold
What a difference would have been in the seeds of life
that were sown
In the years of long ago.

But now we shout with joy
As in the Lord we grow
With our two little girls and one little boy
God holds our future in His Hands
This we truly know!

Written by:

Vada Henson Caldwell

Cynthia Anne Caldwell
August 24, 1948

Thomas H. Caldwell, III
December 24, 1949

Mary Catherine Caldwell
July 8, 1951
In the arms of God November 19, 2012

My Father-In-Law –
Thomas Herbert Caldwell, Sr.
City of Memphis Fireman

In loving memory of

Thomas Herbert Caldwell, Sr.

Beloved Husband, Father, Grandfather and Brother

The year of 1967 has come and gone, and with the passing of this year, the memory of our loss and Heaven's gain will always be in our hearts. May we who are left behind always remember the life gone by and forever live in a way that will insure our meeting again.

He loved the earth, the sky and trees
For he felt closer to God
When surrounded by these.

We children can remember with pride
How he called us to his side
And said, "Promise to take care of your Mother
And always be good to each other."

"My sons, I love you so
And of you have always been proud
Tell all my grandchildren, I want them to know
I have watched them with joy and love through the years.
I've had a good life, so wipe away your tears
And know that I am ready to go."

Oh the wonderful things we have heard. We always knew of his goodness and compassion for others, but it fills our hearts with joy to hear these things from those who knew and worked with him over the years.

Some of the things that were said:

"His quiet goodness was always there. He loved people and people loved him." "Great men are remembered from their services and he lived a good and useful life." Another man said, "Sons, lift your head and smile, because your Dad was a good man."

And still another said, "I worked with him for many years and he never had anything to say against anybody. In all the years I knew him, never, ever have I ever heard a bad word about him. Wouldn't it be wonderful if all could have this said about them?"

And then a young fireman who came to pay his respects shared his feelings with us in these words, "He was my first friend when I went to work for the fire department. Back then they only gave you a duck bill cap and badge. You had to buy your own clothes. Two hours after I started to work we had a bad fire and he gave me part of his clothes to wear. Things like this you never forget.

And then one of the most heartwarming things shared with us was told by our minister and friend. The preacher said, "Your Dad was a man that entered my heart. You know we preachers have a game of picking out those in the congregation who are listening. Every time I ever looked at your Daddy, I knew he was listening to what I had to say."

We will miss our loved one, oh so much, and yet how great it will be to remember him with such Loving Memories.
Your gentle face and patient smile with sadness we recall
You had a kindly word for each and died beloved by all.

The voice is mute and stilled the heart
That loved us well and true
Ah, bitter was the trial to part
From one so good as you.

You are not forgotten loved one,
Nor will you ever be
As long as life and memory last
We will remember thee.

We miss you now, our hearts are sore,
As time goes by we'll miss you more.
Your loving smile, your gentle face.
No one can fill your vacant place.

The most wonderful thing for us who are left behind, is that we can constantly keep in our mind, he is watching us still and sharing our sorrows and joys.

And we know with his gentle voice he is calling —

Meet me at Heaven's gate —
For with love, I patiently wait.

Written this January 7, 1968,

by Mrs. Thomas H. Caldwell, Jr.

My Talk with God

This morning I awoke at five
I rushed frantically about so I could be on my way.
My first thought was not "it's great to be alive."
But "another day of work and can I make it today?"

Now I know prayer works, beyond a shadow of doubt
For suddenly from somewhere I seemed to hear a shout,
Stop rushing, be glad of this day. Others are beginning to pray.
So quietly I prayed, "God help me to do my part."
And truly at that moment He entered my heart.

As I drove to work, I was filled with pride
For I knew the Lord was right by my side.
I told Him everything word by word
And knew that He really had heard.
I spoke of our friends, family and foe
And told Him my joys along with my woe.
And I asked our Father to be with us all.
To guide and direct us, lest we should fall.

As I talked to our Lord in rhyme, I felt our hearts entwined
And I knew He was listening to each of us at the same time.

I whispered Dear Father, Help us today
To do all that we can in our own way
To try to make this year of our life for Thee to shine
A year of God's favor, "For this is the acceptable time".
And all of a sudden from out of the blue,
God said, "Always, I am with you".
And the song kept ringing in my ear

He could have called ten thousand angels to destroy the world and set
him free. He could have called ten thousand angels, but he died alone
for you and me. So fervently, I daily pray God be with us as we go our
way. Be with us each day of the week. As God's blessing we seek.

Written by Vada Caldwell (1969)

Daddy

Daddy, oh Daddy you're gone
But we know to a heavenly home.
We miss your sweet smile and the song on your lips
When sadness the strings of our heart grips.

We know we must trust in God and His plan,
But it would have been good to hold your hand
As I traveled down the road of life these years
Filled with much joy and even with our tears.

Often I wonder if you can see
This world where we walk around free.
And if you look down from heaven above
Can you feel and know of our love.

Do you know Daddy of mine
The lives lived by those you have left behind?
Will we know you as our own sweet love
When we meet in heaven above?

My memories of you are sweet
And yet there are times I must weep.
I think of the joy my children have missed
For by you they never were kissed.
I've tried to tell them over the years
Of your gentle ways and even that you shed tears.
Daddy, my Daddy I love you so
And were so sad when you had to go.
But this I know within my heart
God took you with him to make a new start.
And released you from your bed of pain
As you whispered his sweet name.

"Blessed Savior Pilot Me" were the last words Mother heard you say
and as sure as there is a God, I know you went to heaven that day.

In loving memory of my Daddy L. D. Henson

Born February 22, 1899 - Died October 2, 1946

Written by Mrs. Thomas H. Caldwell, Jr. February 23, 1969

My Mother and Father,
L.D. and Annie Wilma Henson

About My Daddy

I remember the first time I ever saw my Daddy cry. It was at the death of my cousin Warren Jackson. A mule ran away with him and he fell catching his foot in the harness. He was dragged to death and was only 12 years old.

I watched my Daddy as he looked into the casket, tears flowed freely down his face as he softly whispered, "My little partner."

And again I saw him cry when he picked me up and placed me on his knee. My Daddy was a hunter and raised, trained and sold hunting dogs. In training them he used raccoons by dragging them along a trail for the dogs to hunt. He caught a baby coon on one of his hunts and brought it home to me. I fell in love with the little thing and named him Sambo. He was my pet for a very long time. Then one day my Daddy used him in training and he got away. The dogs caught his scent, found and killed him. Daddy was heartbroken when he had to tell me and he cried with me.

My Daddy was a gentle, loving and caring man. He died from cancer when I was eighteen years old. I have so many wonderful memories of him. I loved him so and miss him still.

Tribute to Mother

Red roses are the symbol of love
God made them in multiple numbers
Also the stars shining brightly above
And many more of our Creators wonders!

In His wonderful love all prevailing
God planned His world for our good
And in His wisdom unfailing
It is certain that He understood.

When He made women for Motherhood
To bring children into the world
And teach them bad from good
So her offspring would be able to see
That truly God made all the heavens and earth
But for each child His greatest creation of worth
Could be no other ---
Than Mother!

Every day of every year –
Not just on this day set aside for others to see.
I declare my love for my Mother so dear
And I thank you Mama for what you mean to me.

Yes, God made all the heavens and earth
And at the time of my birth
He gave me a wonderful mother
Who could not be replaced by another.

Written by Vada Henson Caldwell

A Quiet Afternoon Alone

Have you ever listened to a sermon –
When you did not hear a word?
I have, but the fault was in me
For my mind was on other things you see.

Have you ever prayed a prayer –
And felt it was not heard?
I have, and the fault was all mine
For I prayed, my will God not thine.

Have you ever felt blue and really all alone?
I have, but then one look at the clear blue sky
Made me realize that our blessed Savior did die
For all our many sins to atone.

Have you noticed when you are the only one at home
How the quietness all around makes you feel?
Well, the feeling is there and you do feel alone
But to know God we really must sometimes be still.

God be with me throughout this day I pray
And help me to know and find the way
To be one of thy children from day to day
In all that I do and think and say,

In the quiet, quiet stillness of this afternoon
As I have wandered aimlessly from room to room
Thy presence is here, I can feel you so near
For this I am thankful and know with you, there is nothing to fear.

Help me Father to always be
A fitting example of living for thee
I have found that you can pray without uttering a word
And You in your Heavenly Home have always heard.

Again, I beseech you to hold tight to my hand
As I strive from this day forward to take my stand
For Jesus Christ who died for me
That I might have a home in Heaven with thee.

Written by Mrs. Thomas (Vada) Caldwell, Jr.,
Sunday Afternoon, May 25, 1969

Our Son Thomas H. Caldwell, III

Thursday Afternoon June 26, 1969

Every day I've searched the mail
And every day to no avail
For each day there is not a letter from my son
I hope he is well and having some fun.

Perhaps he thought, "My Mother I will repay
Because she stopped writing me every day."
Please let us hear from you
And write us a line or two.

I'm sorry my letters were so few
And promise once again each day to write you
God bless you and keep you my son
For we love you and miss you everyone.

Tonight your sisters play a game of ball
It's too bad you cannot be here
To watch them and urge them on with your call
Because it would help them to hear a big cheer.

Daddy is upstairs hammering away
working every spare minute of each day.
He wants your sister to live here at home
And not leave us to elsewhere roam.

I am sitting here after earning my day's pay
Writing my son who is so far away,
Hoping he might call or write soon.
May the years fly by that keep us apart I pray
Cause without you, our life is not quite in tune.

Daddy, Cindy, Cathy and I all love you
And would you believe me when I say
Wrinkles and Powder Puff love you too.
I know because they tell me so every day.

The days lessen between the time we will meet again
And oh, how we look forward and plan
To have so much fun and enjoy our time with you
Of this, my son, you can be sure it is true.

Well, I really must go now
For I promised Daddy I would help him somehow
As a carpenter, I'm not very good you know
But maybe just being with him will help the room grow
For he wants to hurry and finish the work he has planned
So there will be time for some rest on his hands.

God be with you and keep you every day.
Write soon and remember for us to pray.
And if God be willing, may we soon be with each other.
This is the prayer of your loving Mother.

Mrs. Vada H. Caldwell

My Sister

It seems there is always miles between us
And time daily races on by
I often wonder if it was meant to be thus
And many times reminisce and cry.

I hope all of you are happy and gay
As you go about each busy day,
It would be nice to hear from you
And know that you miss us too.

The world of today seems to be upside down
And causes so many people just to frown,
But thanks to God every once in a while
The world is graced with a beautiful smile.

The love and closeness of families should not be forgotten
And allowed to be always down-trodden.
The world rushes on and on
Then all of a sudden someone you love is gone.

I have a nephew named Roy
Who is a fine Christian boy
Whom you have trained well.

It's wonderful always to hear
When someone desires to live for God
Especially when it is someone so dear
As down the road of life they trod.

You all mean so much to me
I love you and hope all with you is well.
We would welcome a visit from you it's true,
So why don't you come stay for a spell?

It is really a crime
That we never get to be with each other
May God bless you, I pray
And keep you safe both night and day.

Vada Caldwell – June 26, 1969

They that Sow in Tears

They that sow in tears, shall reap in joy.   Psalm 126:5

As we realize the cruel death our Savior suffered for us, we are moved to tears of sadness and grief; yet are filled with joy beyond comparison in the knowledge that we have a blessed Savior to love us and be with us always. Life with Him eternally is ours just for the asking. Jesus knocks at our hearts door and waits patiently to be invited in.

'As I Survey the Wondrous Cross' tears flow freely. When I see the beauty of God's creation, see the upheld hand of a little child, hear a message in song or word, or witness the tears of others my tears flow. Throughout my life when tears have come to my eyes and into my heart, I have been reminded of the scripture, "The Spirit itself beareth witness with our spirit, that we are the children of God." And it is in humble love and gratitude that I thank my God for His presence felt in my life through tears of joy, pride, shame, humility and sorrow.

It is in sharing with others the sorrow of knowing how Jesus suffered in death for us that tears flow. Thru these tears we realize our salvation was made possible through the suffering of my Jesus and His death upon the Cross.

For God so loved the world that He gave His only begotten son, that whosoever believeth in Him should not perish but have everlasting life." John 3:16

By sharing this wonderful message of God's Amazing Love and sowing the precious seed of tears:

We shall reap the Joy … of the Joyful Abundant Life found through Victory in Jesus.

Heavenly Father, I thank you for your Son Jesus who came to live, die and rise again that we might be saved … in His Precious Name.   Amen!

Vada H. Caldwell (March 15, 1969)

Dear God, Hear My Prayer

Dear God, I pray be with me throughout this day and forevermore.

Be with my daughters and their husbands wherever they are.
My earnest prayer is that you have indeed entered their hearts and will keep
them true to their faith with you and each other.

Help me Father to know what to do. Only you know how I have
worried and the heaviness of my heart can only be lifted by Thee.
Before I think or write a sentence you know what is in my heart.

Father take their hands in Thine
Bless their lives with joy sublime.
Let them hear thy voice o'er and o'er
And know thou art just outside the door.

Father let me from this day
Lead them to Thee as I pray.
As I have asked you in the past
Enter their hearts and hold on tight
So they too shall Thy hand clasp
With all their strength and might.

Oh, Dear God I pray
Guide my loved one's day by day.
Help me Father to hold tight too
For Dear God, I need you.

Written by: Vada H. Caldwell – 1970

Have you not read that he which made them at the beginning made
them male and female. And said for this cause shall a man leave father
and mother, and shall cleave to his wife; and they twain shall be one
flesh? Wherefore they are no more twain but one flesh. What therefore
God hath joined together, let not man put asunder. Matthew 19: 4-6

James Phillip Giles

To our golden haired boy
With eyes of blue
Over the years you were our pride and joy
Only God in His heaven knows how we miss you.

Eyes a twinkle and a smile on your face
Some live on this earth and leave not a trace.
Yet you our own with your eyes aglow
Lived in a way that the whole world will know.

Your life on earth to our lives brought cheer
And your memory we all hold so dear.
Oh Phil, our Phil in your Heavenly rest,
Look down on us left below
And know that we grieve because we loved you so.

Today, we all pledge once again
From this day forward to live in a way
That God will unite us all one day
With you our little man.

There is an emptiness now that you are gone,
Comforting is our knowledge that you now abide
With God in His heavenly home
Our own precious joy and pride.

Written in loving memory by Vada Henson Caldwell (February 1, 1970)

Friends

The days seem long
As we trod along
Yet still tis great
That old master fate
has let our paths cross
For a friend such as you today
cannot be counted a loss.
Cause your smiles help
all along the way.

Written by Vada Caldwell – August 14, 1970

We

My husband, my love, my all
For some reason today these words I recall.
June 15, 1946 we said "till death do us part"
With a song of joy in our heart.

We have traveled together along the road of life
For almost twenty-three wonderful years
As father, mother, husband and wife
We've shared sickness, health, laughter and tears.

We've watched our children as they have grown
From babies to young adulthood
And oh, the great places we've been and the things we've done
There's nothing I would change even if I could.

Now they have all reached the point in their life
Where they must make a start on their own
If only we could spare them all their troubles and strife
That someday they will have to meet
Is the cry that comes from deep within
And yet to deny them their right to overcome all this and win
Would really be accomplishing nothing but their defeat.
For learning from experience as they grow, I have always known
Is really God's plan in life.

During the years 1967 through 1970 so many changes were brought, three
graduations, two weddings and a life in the Navy for our boy.
As a mother, these changes made me overwrought
As we watched our children's graduation from high school
My heart swelled with pride.
And I knew for the Navy our son would soon leave

And this I must be able to accept with the Lord by my side.
For he had grown into manhood which was hard for me to believe.

He is no longer a bundle of joy,
To hold close in my arms
But a young man, instead of a boy.
So I whispered, Dear God keep him from harm.

And on August 19, 1968 he left to serve his country as a sailor.
Before leaving for the airport to see him depart
He said, "Now Mother don't you shed a tear".
Every boy has to give four years or else be a failure.

So bravely I kissed him goodbye with a smile
With my heart breaking inside all the while
When the plane had disappeared into the sky
Then in your arms I truly did cry.

Oh God, Dear God, we love him so
Please be with him wherever he may go.
Always hold him close in your hand
And never let him forget for Christ to stand.

Then Cindy, our first born came to me and said,
Mama I want to get married to Ron
He had wooed her and her heart won!
But Lord she's so innocent and just a sweet child
Can't I please keep her with me for just a little while?
But it wasn't meant to be, the Wedding Day was set
Plans were made, and the two became one.

On June 9, 1970 Cindy and Ron were joined together with God's
blessings and became husband and wife.
A more beautiful bride I have never seen.
Our daughter erect as a queen
And the groom was so proud
As he said, "I do" out loud.
And you know it's true at the wedding the mother always cries.

The next thing I knew, Cathy our youngest came to me and said,
I've met the boy I want to wed.
Once again I prayed,
Dear God she is so innocent and just a sweet child
Can't I please keep her with me for just a little while?

But fate would have it otherwise
The Wedding Date was set and planned.
Another beautiful bride with our love all around, one more beautiful could not
be found.

Our last child was leaving home
And you, my love and I were left alone.

As the brides and grooms went on their way --
I felt the need and began to pray.
Dear Lord, forever let their hearts entwine
And their hands hold tightly to thine.

There once was only you and me
Then Cindy came along and made our number three
Then God blessed us with a son and made us four
And another girl Cathy added to our number one more.

And truly we can say today
God has blessed us all the way.
And we will always have our love for each other.
Husband, wife, sisters and brother.

We must never forget
How great it is to be alive
As we patiently wait for what God has for us yet.

We thank Thee God for all Thy love
And pray we will be worthy to live with Thee above.

Written in love and sadness and gladness and thankfulness by

Mrs. Thomas H. Caldwell, Jr. (December, 1970)

Our Family Tommy, Jr., Vada, Tommy III,
Cindy and Cathy Caldwell

Tommy, Vada, Tommy III,
Cathy and Cindy

Cathy, Vada, Cindy,
Tommy and Tommy III

Is Your Choice Worthwhile?

Whether said in poetry or prose –
That Jesus Christ is the One you've chose,
Over and above all.
Be the opportunity either great or small,
Tis wonderful to share the news,
And ask others, who do you choose?

Written by Mrs. (Vada) Thomas Caldwell, Jr. (November 27, 1971)

Daily Living

Dear Father in Heaven, I pray.
Help me to know what to say,
As I live from day to day.
Please keep me from faltering along the way.

My life and all I have, to Thee I give
And pledge henceforth to always live
As Thou wouldst have me do.
Lord my strength must come from you.

Praise God in Heaven above,
For His undying love.
He gave you, His beloved Son
For the sins of all the world, one by one.

Written by Mrs. Vada Caldwell

Praise Be to God!

Thank you Jesus, for saving my soul,
And from the bonds of sin I have been set free,
Through the love of God I have been made whole,
Hallelujah and praise be unto Thee!

Thank you Jesus, for being my friend,
And letting me know that in spite of my unworthiness
Your love is real, oh so real and not pretend,
Hallelujah and praise be for Thy loving kindness.

Thank you Jesus, for giving to me
The joy of life and privilege of living for Thee.
Yes, thank you Jesus and may others always see
Thy loving hand in all that I will ever be.

Praise God for sending His son to earth,
To live and walk the roads of Galilee;
That all who believed in His lowly birth
And His death on Calvary's tree,
Might live forever in Heaven with Thee.

Written by Mrs. Vada K. Caldwell
Dedicated to a beloved friend in Jesus Name, December 1, 1971

Use Me Lord God

Oh, Lord my God
I call unto thee for all
Praise God, the Lord of Hosts

Take me this day and use me Lord for your glory.
Hide me oh my Savior behind the Cross.
Let every word coming from my mouth be music to your ears.

Oh Lord I humbly pray, let all the things I do, be done for Thee.
Take this day and me now Lord and make us Thine!

Written by Vada Caldwell (1973)

Youth and Life

It was thirty years ago when first we met
And aye tis sure we'll never forget
The girlhood dreams we shared
And the vows together we oft declared
Lifelong friends we'll always be
Me for you and you for me!

And now with eyes dimmed by tears
The question comes to my mind…
What happened to all those years?
They have all slipped by and fell behind.

The time has flown rapidly by, and yet
It seems only yesterday we shared our dreams
And talked about our future amid life's many schemes.
These things, we will never forget.

We pledged in those days of our past
Always to care and keep in touch
Promised that our love for each would last
Hoping our paths would not separate too much.

When I look back at the "good old days"
It is apparent that in so many, many ways
Our lives came through some stormy weather,
For times of both joy and sadness we met together.

Those days of our lives were spent in study, play and living
Words spoken hastily and unkindly were always easily forgiven.
As down the road of life we walked, it seemed so slow
The years were passing along and we didn't even know
That the days of our youth were stored up treasure
And would in our minds forever be remembered with pleasure.

Although the days of our girlhood have passed. Our love and
friendship has continued to last. I know it's true, so very true
My life has been better for having met you.

Written by Vada Henson Caldwell (November, 1973)

A poem my Lord gave me in answer to a prayer, especially for
Lona Lovett Roberts, for her birthday November 13th.

Lord, give me a poem for Lona, I pray
Let me tell her what I feel within my heart
It seems to me like only yesterday
When we were never found apart.

Memphis Fairgrounds October 1, 1944

*Lona Lovett &
Vada Henson*

My Son Tommy and me,
Vada Caldwell, Leaving for
Navy

Thomas H. Caldwell, III
Navy Whites

Tommy Navy Jacket

I Remember Christmas

One Christmas Eve my life was blessed with wealth untold
In the birth of a baby boy, a joy to behold.
With joy I watched him grow; this son of mine
A daily reminder of our Christmas in 1949

The time came when I had to say goodbye.
He said, "Now, Mother don't you dare cry".
So bravely I kissed him with a smile.
As I watched the plane disappear into the sky.
My brave spirit gave way to despair
The tears flowed freely, for my son was no longer there.

He was no longer a bundle of joy
To cuddle and hold close in my arms.
But a young man instead of a boy
So I whispered, Dear Lord keep him from harm.

The Navy took the young boy who held my hand
And as he traveled across the sea
They quickly changed him into a man
No longer a child dependent upon me.

As the days, months and years passed
Anxiously we awaited the day he would be home at last.
Letters came from far away, Brazil, Manila, and Singapore
Bangladesh and then the Vietnam shore.

One cold December night in 1972
Answering a gentle knock on the door, I saw standing there
A tall young man with curly hair and bearded face
As he greeted me with a smile and a strong embrace
The joy in my heart was beyond compare
for once again for Christmas, God blessed me with a son.

Yes, I remember Christmas - - not just one but two.
I remember - - every day all year through.

Written by Vada Caldwell (December, 1973)

My Son Tommy Caldwell and wife, Tammie

Tommy & Tammie Caldwell

Sam Caldwell Sheppard,
Russell Blake Caldwell,
Lorrie Beth Caldwell Leach

A Better Way

Little did I know when I saw you standing by the road
That you were a soul in deep need of a friend,
And yet something said that you were carrying a heavy load
I knew just then a helping hand I must extend.

Oh, how sad this world is today
when we see someone along the way,
Someone in need of help from a passerby
and fear keeps us from helping, oh why, oh why?

Surely our world could be a better place
If all would realize we are God's human race.
Slow down and look around as you go from day to day
Yes, God is there to show us a better way.

If only we open our hearts, our minds, and our ears
Live our lives for Jesus just one day or a minute at a time
Rejoice now and worry not about the future years
But pray for the Holy Spirit to keep us within God's will divine
Just trust in the indwelling spirit to see that God's will we find.

Vada H. Caldwell (1974)

Help Me Dear Lord

Good morning Lord in this quiet hour
The best time of the day.
While alone with Thee I humbly pray
To be filled with Thy love, spiritual
courage and power.

Help me oh Lord throughout the day
To witness for Thee along the way.
Thank you Dear Lord for all you've done
Thank you for giving your only son.

And thank you Dear Jesus
for saving the world and
a wretch like me.

Praise God, the Father and the Son.

Written by Vada Caldwell (February 24, 1974, 6:30 A.M.)

Try Me Lord

Try me oh Lord, try me, I cry
Try my patience, my faith, my love
And still, oh God I'll praise Thee
As my everlasting strength from above.

Oh blessed Lord, I praise Thy name
For all my trials, troubles and sorrows
For all the mental and physical strain
For Dear God in your hands are all our tomorrows.

As we travel the paths of life, You and I
Whatever we meet along the way
I'll accept as Thy precious will from day to day
And continue to love Thee while awaiting the
Sweet by and by.

Thank you Lord, for helping me grow
By giving me trials to make me feel low
And showing me how to hold on to Thee
So my burdens will be lifted and my troubled
Spirit made free.

Dear God, I humbly call out to you
The days have been filled with troubled times
And I simply could not have made it through
Had it not been for Thy love and the blessed
Assurance that Jesus is mine!

Thank you Jesus, for being near
And protecting those I hold dear.
For guiding my footsteps all the way
Praise God, I feel Thy presence every day.

Try me, Oh Lord, I cry
And I'll trust you o'er and o'er
Praise God, Jesus came to save a sinner such as I.
So we could meet on Eternity's Shore.

Written by: Mrs. Vada Henson Caldwell (June, 1974)

Praise God

Yes, Praise God for all blessings, but then pray,
Oh, God give me a burden to bring others to know Christ.
The Bible teaches us to Praise God all the time and in
everything to give thanks.

As we live our life from day to day
Let us not forget to pray for others
And to ask God to help us to help others to come to know
Jesus as their Savior.

Thank you Lord for making me whole,
But give my heart a burden Lord
To win for you another soul.

Thank you Lord for the joy to me you gave
But give me a burden Lord, give me a burden I pray,
That I might go forth in your name and pray
So those who are lost might be saved.

Let us all be of one accord and pray that God will
burden all Christians to win souls for His Kingdom.

Written by Vada Caldwell (August 5, 1974)

The Master's Touch

This morning as I sat quietly in the early hours of the day, all asleep in the house but me. After a period of Bible reading and meditation in a moment of quiet with my God, in prayer I turned my face toward Heaven. Oh Dear Lord touch me today I prayed.

My eyes came to rest on a stained crack on the ceiling. I remembered that when the house was first built, with the first rain, the roof was found to be leaking. The builder was contacted and the roofing company came out and repaired the roof. The leak was no longer there. However, we did not call the sheetrock man to return.

As I looked at this spot on my living room ceiling, I thought; this imperfection could no longer be seen if only we had called the sheetrock man to come back. All it needed to be covered properly was the touch of a master's hand.

Then my heart rejoiced with the knowledge that our mistakes and imperfections can be covered by the saving grace and precious blood of Jesus, our Master.

I raised my voice in prayer.
Our Most Gracious Heavenly Father, hallowed be Thy name. How I praise you Dear God for your Beloved Son – our Savior and Redeemer.

AMEN.

Written by Vada Henson Caldwell – (1974)

The Value of a Smile

When you feel that things are really tough
And you have an extra heavy load,
Just put a smile upon your face and bear it.
You will find there are those along the road
Ready to see your need and willing to share it.

A face marked with an ugly frown
Dampens the spirits of those around.
A smile not only brightens a person's face,
It lightens the way for the human race.

Written by Vada Caldwell (September 19, 1975)

Love

If love could be measured,
We would tell you how much we love you.
Your love for us and our love for you should be treasured
And that is just what we will always do.

For all of our yesterdays with you
We will be thankful to our Father in Heaven above
And share with others, the rivers of love
You have given us all these years through.

You have shown us that we are never alone
And that Jesus reigns on His throne.
You have served Him well and the message taught
By the precious blood of Jesus, we have been bought.

You have fed us the Word of God for seven wonderful years
You have led us into a closer walk with Jesus in laughter and in tears.
You have taught us the message of sorrow
It was for us, Jesus was nailed to the cross
That we might have abundant life and the joy of tomorrow.

As we remember our years with you
And realize that seven is God's perfect number,
We know the Lord Himself stood by you.
And we pledge to you and our God, we will not slumber.
I can hear our Savior now as He says to you
Well done, my good and faithful servant … you have been true.
And we know with God's help we will keep on growing.
For you have given us good measure, pressed down and
overflowing.

Written by Mrs. Vada Caldwell June 2, 1978

In honor of our Pastor and friend, Edna and Elwood Thornton.

They will never be forgotten and we shall always love them and thank God for the

years we had together.

Give of Yourself for the Master

When we are willing to give of ourselves for the Glory of God – always we will receive rich dividends in abundance. Once this giving of oneself is made – total giving of self for God and others – we are never the same again.

Throughout life as we give ourselves for God and others we grow into bigger and better people. As we share our love for Christ and our faith in Him with others – then that love and faith grows within us.

As we come in contact with others day by day we find more and more ways to give of ourselves. These encounters we have every day show us the need for more study in our life === so our knowledge of God's Word will grow. As our knowledge grows === then our love grows and we have a deeper and closer walk with God.

Lord, help me to grow.

Written by Vada Caldwell (August 3, 1978, At Work 9:00 PM)

Christmas

Christmas to me means many things. The warmth of love in the air, the beauty of the world our Lord has made. The peace and happiness of a wonderful home, the blessings of a loving family. The joy and wealth of having friends in my life.

Most of all Christmas means to me the glorious joy of the birth of a babe in the manger, and deep sorrow that He had to die for the salvation of all mankind. My heart is filled with humble gratitude for this precious gift of God.

Christmas rings out with the message – Glory to God in the highest! Peace on earth, good will to men!

Prayerfully and joyfully I ask God His blessings to impart.

With all my heart, I wish you CHRISTMAS!

From the heart of Vada Henson Caldwell

December 12, 1978

Reflections from My Heart from the First Letter of the Alphabet

And God said unto Moses, I <u>Am</u> that I <u>Am</u>. (Exodus 3:14)

We are told in Deut. 6:5 and Mark 12:30 that our <u>affections</u> should be supremely set upon God.

<u>Abba</u> (Father) sent His Son for the <u>atonement</u> of our sins that we might have Jesus as our <u>anchor</u> in life and through faith have <u>assurance</u> of life everlasting.

We are <u>admonished</u> to live for Christ, to <u>admit</u> our sins, to <u>accept Christ</u> as King of our lives. The <u>abundant affection</u> of our Lord Jesus is manifested in ways unnumbered. We read in I John 2:1 that we have an <u>advocate</u> with the Father Jesus Christ the righteous:

If we <u>abide</u> in Him and He in us. . .we will give <u>alms</u> (love) unto our brother who is in need. For he who loves God…loves his brother also. (I John 3)

We have the wonderful privilege of becoming <u>ambassadors</u> for Christ and as we read and remember the scripture found in Matthew 28:20. . . "Lo, I am with you always then we can <u>affirm</u> our <u>assurance</u> with a resounding <u>Amen</u> and Amen!

Written with Love,
Vada Caldwell
July 20, 1979

Thoughts of Reflection

What are some important words in the Bible beginning with the letter "R"? How do they relate to the life of a Christian? Reflection, Rest, Repentance, Restoration, Reward, Redemption, Remember, Release, Resist.

Perhaps this would be an interesting exercise...think on the letters of the alphabet, think of words beginning with the letters which apply to the Christian life and explain how. A method of study and thought you might find . . . Rewarding.

My thoughts on the words above beginning with the letter "R".   May you find the message interesting and thought provoking.

The greatest restoration is that of one who has sinned and been restored through redemption, received by true repentance and release of that sin through Jesus Christ.

A reward of the knowledge that God will remember your sin no more.

As perceived and written by,

Vada Henson Caldwell

April 20, 1979

Power of Prayer

Thoughts shared from the heart of Mrs. Vada Caldwell on Prayer, August 24, 1980.

Throughout the teachings of the Bible, we read of the importance of Prayer. Prayer is our door to conversation with Christ. We are told to "Ask and Ye shall receive", "Knock and it shall be opened unto you". We must pray, we must knock and ask our Lord for His guidance daily.

When we are troubled, in doubt or have decisions to make …we find that prayer is what keeps us going.

In reading the Bible we find Prayer to be the way to receive God's help. Prayer is not just reciting some words that we put together. We must live, breathe and believe as we pray. To receive God's guidance we must work at our prayer. We must be in earnest and mean what we say. We must ask, Christ is there waiting for us to ask him and he will give unto us as we believe. When Jesus said "knock and it shall be opened unto you," He meant just that, and we can never know how much real comfort and aid can be received until we really lean on Jesus and learn to PRAY.

What is PRAYER? It is the bridge over which man can speak to the Almighty. It is just simply talking to our creator, our Savior, our Lord and Master.

In a quiet time of reflection, looking deep within ourselves and searching for guidance, we feel the presence of Christ. He will hear and He will answer…as we knock, believe and … be still and know that He is God.

May God bless each of us as we pray for ourselves and each other.

What is Life?

Life is filled with broken dreams
And driving, relentless schemes.
The search for all we've lost
At such a tremendous cost.

This world of ours today
Needs urgently to pray.
The old and young are all uptight.
Is it the dread that death might come in the night?

If only we, throughout each hectic day
Could hear our Savior say - -
All you are and all you have is mine,
Just let your life for me always shine.
You'll see life can be fulfilled dreams
And carefree, enriching schemes.

As we truly lift our voices in prayer and song,
We see our thoughts have all been wrong.
For things we thought of as loss,
Must be counted as but dross.
Our Savior Jesus Christ died on the cruel Cross,
that both you and I might live.
So for every lamentation of our life, we should whisper,
"Lord, forgive."

And each heart filled with prayer,
Praising God, that He did care
Enough to make His Son pay the cost,
That we today, might be saved instead of lost!

With God's Love and Mine,

Vada Caldwell

September 5, 1979

My Grandchild

AN ANGEL FACE FRAMED BY GOLDEN CURLS
BIG BLUE EYES SPEAK WITH OUTSTANDING EXPRESSION
A TOUCH OF HER HAND,
A SMILE FROM HER LIPS
A PRECIOUS JEWEL FORMED BY GOD'S OWN HAND.

HER TINY HAND IN MINE
BRINGS A TUG AT MY HEART
AND JOY TO MY LIFE
THANK YOU DEAR GOD FOR MY
LORRIE BETH!

Written by:

Vada Caldwell

April 2, 1982

Lorrie Beth Caldwell Leach

Born May 24, 1979

In the arms of God

September 18, 2014

Lorrie Beth and Brother Russell Caldwell

Lorrie Beth

Grandaddy
Thomas H.
Caldwell with baby
granddaughter
Lorrie Beth

Lorrie Beth
& her Dad
Tommy Caldwell

Sam, Lorrie Beth &
Russell Caldwell

Baby Lorrie Beth and
Big Sister Sam Caldwell

This Is the Time

This is the hour to call upon God
As upon this earth you trod,
Your every need our God will meet
If only you kneel at His feet.
And as you truly seek His face,
All your sins He will erase.

His open arms are beckoning you
Come, my child, to me be true.
I died on the cross, that you might live
Just ask and I'll forgive.

In heaven for you, I have prepared a place
If only for me, you will run life's race.

Vada H. Caldwell

August 23, 1982

As this year draws to a close, and a New Year appears over the horizon let us think on special moments of life with special meanings. Thoughts from the pen of Vada Caldwell, 1982.

In this Special Moment of Life

THINK FREELY. PRACTICE PATIENCE.
SMILE OFTEN. SAVOR SPECIAL MOMENTS.
LIVE GOD'S MESSAGE. MAKE NEW FRIENDS.
DISCOVER OLD ONES. TELL THOSE YOU LOVE THAT YOU DO.
FEEL DEEPLY. FORGET TROUBLE. FORGIVE AN ENEMY.
HOPE. GROW. BE CRAZY AND FORGET WORRY.
COUNT YOUR BLESSINGS. OBSERVE MIRACLES.
MAKE THEM HAPPEN. GIVE. GIVE IN. TRUST ENOUGH TO TAKE.
PICK SOME FLOWERS. SHARE THEM.
KEEP A PROMISE. LOOK FOR RAINBOWS. GAZE AT THE STARS.
WORK HARD. BE WISE. TRY TO UNDERSTAND.
TAKE TIME FOR PEOPLE. TAKE TIME FOR YOURSELF.
LAUGH HEARTILY. SPREAD JOY. SEE BEAUTY EVERYWHERE.
TAKE A CHANCE. REACH OUT. LET SOMEONE IN.
TRY SOMETHING NEW. SLOW DOWN. BE SOFT SOMETIMES.
BELIEVE IN YOURSELF. TRUST OTHERS. SEE A SUNRISE.
LISTEN TO RAIN. REMINISCE. CRY WHEN YOU NEED TO.
TRUST LIFE. HAVE FAITH. ENJOY WONDER.
COMFORT A FRIEND. HAVE GOOD IDEAS.
MAKE SOME MISTAKES. LEARN FROM THEM.
LIVE GOD'S MESSAGE. CELEBRATE LIFE.

Hear Me, Oh Lord My God

Oh Lord my God I cry
From the depth of my soul
Why, Oh Lord Why
Does my heart ache to find console?
Help me, Dear God I pray
Please show me again the way
You would have me to go
For I do truly love you so.

Remove from my heart all doubt
And help me, Oh God to proclaim with a shout
You and you alone can save my soul
And make me whole!

Come Holy Spirit, flow into my being
Fill me with peace and love.
I know this comes only from above
And I ask to receive, with a heart of believing!

Written by:

Vada Caldwell – 1984

Oh Lord My God

Thank you Jesus for saving my soul
Keep me safe in Thy tender care.
Through Thee, I have been made whole
For life eternal with Thee, I now prepare,

Open my heart, my soul, my mind
As Thy precious promises I find
Help me Lord, give me eyes to see
That I might lead others to Thee.

Oh Lord, my glorious God
While here on earth I trod,
May my footprints shape a path to Thee
And may others see Jesus in me.

Guide me through every day
Use me Lord, I pray.

Vada Caldwell

September, 1984

A Burdened Heart

Thank you, Lord for making me whole.
But give my heart a burden Lord,
Give my heart a burden.

Thank you Lord for the Joy I have
But burden my heart to give it away Lord
to give it away!

Give me a burden Lord,
Give me a burden I pray
To help show others the way.

My love for You is strong
Please help me to do no wrong.
Mold me and make me after Thy Will
While I am watching, waiting and still.

Vada Caldwell - 1986

Peace Be Still

Amid the busy sounds of the world
The voice of God can be heard.
As He whispers to me, Peace Be Still
Calmness oe'r my being I feel
For I trust in His Holy Word.

Inner peace God will to you impart
If only His presence you seek.
Say, Lord of all come into my heart.
Listen, you will hear Him speak.

Be thou still, Child of Mine
Draw near to me one day at a time.
Lean on me, I'll see you through
My strength and my peace I give to you.

Written by:

Vada Henson Caldwell

December 30, 1986

Seize Every Moment

Each day as the sun begins to rise
And I view the earth, the trees, the skies
I find myself upon my knees
Thanking our Lord for the moment to seize.

Seize the moment to live
Live each day to the fullest degree
Seize the moment to give
Give of yourself whenever the need you see.

Seize the moment to live, to work and play
Enjoy life all through the day
Share the joy and sorrow of others
Extend a hand to your sisters and brothers.

Seize the moment to say "I love you"
To your mate, so good and true.
Take time to watch the grandchildren play
Stop and listen to what they have to say.

Plant a flower, climb a tower
Touch the ground, look all around.
Take a walk in the rain
Praise His Holy Name.

Seize every moment to Praise God and pray
Thanking Him throughout each day
For the time to live, give, work and play.

Written by Vada Henson Caldwell

January, 1987

The Amazing Eagle

The Eagle is a majestic sight to watch as she soars through the sky. The mother eagle cares for her young, just as your mother cares for you.

When a baby is born, for a time the baby does not know how to walk. When you become old enough to try your first step, your mother either holds you by the hand or stands behind with her hands outstretched to catch you if you should fall.

The mother eagle builds her nest high above the ground and brings her babies food every day. When the baby eagle becomes strong enough to fly … The mother eagle gently pushes the baby from the nest.

As she watches her baby tumbling thru the air, she swoops down beneath her baby with wings outstretched making a wind to lift her baby and keep it from falling.

Just as the mother eagle is the wind beneath the wings of the baby eagle loving and caring for her child . . . So our God is beneath each one of us ready to catch us if we fall.

God is always with us, loving and protecting us with His amazing and wonderful power. We can always trust God because He will never leave us.

Written by: Vada Caldwell

1989

The Majesty of God's World

I retired from Kellogg Company the last of April in 1990 and began a new routine. On July 16, 1990 while cleaning the windows in the sunroom, I saw something magnificent that I had never seen before.

A tiny little creature flew by the window and landed on the landscaping timbers bordering the flower beds. For a moment, my eyes drank in the beauty of this unusual sight. Excitedly, I called, "Lorrie Beth! Russell! Come quickly!" As we looked out the window, I said, "Look at that tiny little creature. Its wings look like four little flags." My 11-year-old granddaughter Lorrie Beth said, It's a dragonfly, Mamaw."

I told them it was so unusual looking that I wanted them to see it. I asked Russell, my six-year-old grandson if he had seen one before, and his answer was yes. "Look," I said with excitement, "the body looks like a miniature toy sword." As we watched, another flew by, then another, and another.

Hurriedly I found my camera and went outside. Lorrie Beth and Russell stayed inside to watch. Slowly and quietly, I crept closer and closer to the flower bed. Fearing they would fly away if I moved closer, I raised the camera, took the picture, and then took another.

It is such a joy to view the world through the eyes of a child. That day, I made a marvelous discovery – a dragonfly has four square wings and a tiny gray sword-shaped body. At the age of 62, I experienced the delight of the child deep within.

Written by: Mrs. Vada Caldwell

July, 1990

Christmas Day, 1990

The scene from my kitchen window this morning is one of solitude and tranquility. Standing still and naked is a forest of trees in every shape and size. The green holly and cedar trees here and there and the falling snow lends a touch of softness to their stark beauty.

The bird feeders hanging from tree limbs and some attached to the massive trunks are surrounded by a flurry of activity. Bright red Cardinals, Blue Jays, Wrens, Sparrows, Wood Thrushes and even a few woodpeckers. Each one adds a brilliance of color to the scene.

As I watch these beautiful little feathered friends. I see our bushy tailed visitors scurrying from tree to tree and limb to limb and finally into the largest feeder on the tree trunk. Their busy little feet and hands send the seeds falling onto the blanket of snow below. Soon the ground is covered with birds hopping from place to place, leaving their tiny footprints as evidence they had been there.

A feeling of peace fills my being and I think how thankful I am for this blessed experience of joy. What a glorious sight of God's creation.

In the valley below smoke curls from the chimney of our son's home. My heart quickens with love as my thoughts turn to the family in this house safe from harm and cradled in warmth and love. Our son Tommy, daughter-in-law Nancy, three beloved grandchildren, Sam, Lorrie Beth and Russell. Their love for us adds blessings to our life.

Our first born, a precious daughter Cynthia Anne brings great joy to our life. Today, I think of our Cindy, her husband Ron, our three beloved grandchildren Ronnie, Johnny and Pamela living in our neighbor state of Mississippi. Though we are separated by miles our love forever binds us together.

Our youngest child, a beautiful daughter, Mary Catherine and our two granddaughters Amy and Becky bring joy to our hearts. Though they too are separated from us by miles we are together in spirit.

My beloved husband Tommy and I have shared almost 45 years together. Over the years we have had our struggles and our triumphs, times of joy and sorrow. Days filled with hope and love. Our lives have been blessed beyond measure.

I thank our God every day for our beautiful family, one by one. All precious and cherished treasures to have and to hold all the days of our lives.

From the heart of

Vada Henson Caldwell

My Grandson Ronnie

Ronald Harold Pritchard, Jr.
United States Marine

Written in honor of my grandson as he was leaving to return to military duty.

My Grandson Ronnie

My mind raced into the realm of despair
As I watched your plane vanish in the air.
That evening I closed my eyes and said a prayer.
Sleep escaped me as I lay there.

My thoughts of you as I recalled our goodbye embrace
And wondering when again I will see your face.
Oh Ronnie, my grandson I love you so.
To just what extent you'll never know.

As a baby small I held you in my arms
And prayed dear God keep him from all harm.
I held your hand when you began to walk
And laughed with joy when I first heard you talk.

Oh the happiness you brought our way
As we watched you grow day by day.
And now beloved you are a young man.
It's time to take your life in hand.

As you travel the road of life every day.
It's now up to you to choose the way.

Know I love you and always will.
Daily asking God to guide and keep you in His will.
Go forth dear one, decide what you want to do
And do it, do it just for you.

Your loving grandmother

Written January 21, 1991

Our church planned an Easter sunrise worship service on Easter morning, April 19, 1992, and invited all the churches in the community to join us. My pastor asked me to share my testimony of faith. I agreed but was nervous about it so I prayed asking God to tell me what to say. Standing on a hillside overlooking a beautiful lake on that glorious Easter morning, God spoke to me. I began my testimony:

As I thought of what I would say this morning to share my faith with you, I was reminded of verse 15 in the third chapter of I Peter. "Be ready always to give an answer to every man that asketh you a reason of the hope that is in you."

"I believe in the risen Christ and stand in awe of his majesty, his power and redeeming love. He has blessed me with his presence in times of joy and sorrow. He has held my hand as we walked the road of life together and carried me in his arms when I have grown weary.

My Lord and Savior has done so much for me, heaping blessings upon blessings and I have done so little for him.

Surrounded by God's mercy, grace and redeeming love, many times throughout the days of my life I have failed my Lord and He continues to love me and bless me over and over.

I believe in the power of prayer. I believe our Savior is interested in every part of our lives and is ready to answer the smallest request and lift the heaviest burden. A prayer that the rain would be held back for just a brief time, a prayer that He would let me feel and know His presence is with me, and a prayer for the healing of a loved one.

I know that I will never be worthy of his touch, his guidance, his presence or his love, and yet as I live each day striving to be what He wants me to be:

I pray for His touch and I feel it, I pray for His guidance and receive it, I pray for others and receive the assurance that my prayer is heard and will be answered."

God gave me a poem as I was preparing this message. The poem really affirms my faith.

My Jesus Loves Me, This I Know!

With broken and contrite heart, I survey the wondrous cross
Filled with sorrow I bow in shame and humbly cry . . .
Why did my Savior die for one such as I?

Then sings my soul
He is my God, my Savior and my all
He has cleansed and made me whole.

In Him I safely hide
He is always by my side
He cheers me when I'm sad
And forgives me when I'm bad

He lifts me when I fall
He hears and answers every call.

Yes, unworthy I'll always be
Even so,
My Jesus died for me!

From the Heart of: Mrs. Thomas (Vada) Caldwell, Jr.

Laity Sunday Message

Book of John Chapter 13:34-35

A new commandment I give unto you, That ye love one another; as I have loved you, that ye also love one another. By this shall all men know that ye are my disciples, if ye have love one to another.

Jesus was speaking to his disciples preparing them for his leaving. He is telling them that their mutual love would be the strongest possible argument for the Christian faith. In chapter 14 he continues to prepare them for the times they will have to face without him. He gives them specific encouragements. The provision of a place in the Father's house, His promise to return, the prospect of doing greater works, the promise of answered prayer, the coming of the Holy Spirit and the legacy of peace.

All of these encouragements apply to us today as well as the new commandment to love one another and the promise that all men will know that we are his disciples, if we have love for one another. (This is not an option it is a command.) We are commanded by Christ to love one another.

The disciples were called to follow Jesus, just as we are today. We are called of God to follow Christ, to witness for him and to proclaim the good news to all men.

Many times I fall short of this calling and sometimes forget the things I should be dwelling and thinking upon. The verse of scripture that helps me to come back into the right perspective with my thoughts and deeds is the 26th verse of John 14. "But the Comforter, which is the Holy Ghost, whom the

Father will send in my name, he shall teach you all things, and bring all things to your remembrance, whatsoever I have said unto you."

Realizing that the Holy Spirit is with us always and the knowledge that God will never leave us helps keep me going day by day.

For the past several weeks on the way to and from work, I have heard a song which speaks to my heart. It goes something like this……

There is a tree out in the back yard
That has never been broken by the wind
And the reason this tree is still standing
Is because it's strong enough to bend.

The words then compare the love of a man and woman to the tree,
And says …Our love will live forever
Just because we are strong enough to bend.

I believe we could also compare the strength of our church to this tree. Each of us here are called of Christ to be his disciples. We have joined hearts, minds and hands over the years to follow this call.

I believe with all my heart that the reason Embury still stands strong casting it's light into the world, is because

WE HAVE ALWAYS HAD THE ABILITY TO LOVE
AND HAVE BEEN WILLING TO BEND.

Written and Spoken By

Mrs. Thomas Caldwell, Jr. (Vada)

Little Things Add to Life

Everyone, at one time or another, finds it difficult just making it from day to day. That is why we have to stop and think. How can we better our life? It is amazing how "little things" can improve the quality of our life and make other people happier, too.

Some of the things we can do to enrich our life and the life of others are "little" and yet so wonderfully valuable. To list only a few:

Share some of your knowledge with someone who needs it!
Eat lunch under a shady tree.
Strike up a conversation with someone you would like to get to know.
Tell someone you appreciate them.
Pick up a book and read it.
Stop and take note of the people around you … they are beautiful.
Look at the lowliest weed, there's beauty in it, too.
Make a point to acquire at least one new bit of knowledge each day.
Clean out your closet and chest of drawers.
Take a different way home.
Try a new food.
Help someone who needs it.
Stop and think about you, your life and what you want to make of it.
Learn to laugh and to cry.
Fill your life with good things.
Practice the "happiness habit" ---- smile!
If you love someone, tell them NOW!

My Daddy always said, "Give me roses while I live." This is something I have always tried to practice.

May God bless each of you all day, every day.

Written by: Mrs. Vada Caldwell

November, 1992

Happenings in Our Life

-by Vada Henson Caldwell

Tommy and I have three children, a son Tommy and two daughters, Cindy and Cathy. We are blessed with eight wonderful grandchildren, Sam, Lorrie Beth, Russell; Ronnie, Johnny, Pamela; Amy and Becky and one precious great grandson Stephen. All through each year we have great times of celebration for birthdays, anniversaries, and holidays. I thank God for our family.

In 1991 from November 15 to December 27, we attended seven funerals of friends and relatives. During the holiday season it seemed even worse to have to give up a loved one. But it certainly brought to my heart and mind how good and gracious is our God who gives us all the strength to cope with the trials of life. And, oh how blessed we are to have had the privilege of knowing those who have gone before.

In September we went to a Mohundro Family Reunion. My grandmother Henson was a Mohundro before her marriage. My Daddy was their first child. At the Mohundro reunion, all of the Henson's there decided we should have a Henson reunion…one cousin said, "I know someone who lives in a big house in the country and it would be a perfect place". She meant our home so Tommy and I said that would be fine with us. We began planning and had the reunion at our house on December 16. We had a wonderful time, children who were cousins and had never seen each other were filled with awe at the news everyone there was their relative. Many of my cousins whom I had not seen since childhood came for the celebration. What a glorious time we had renewing our bonds of love and reaching out to our past and bringing the family into a full circle once again.

My Precious Little Mamaw Lizzie Mohundro Henson

A Special time of celebration for the Family of: Zolicoffer Henson and Elizabeth Mohundro Henson. The parents of my father, L.D. Henson

Miracle of Healing

Slowly, slowly, slowly
The sun began to rise
Illuminating the skies
With all of God's glory.

Slowly, slowly, slowly
The pain began to subside
God's Love Revealing
His Power of miraculous healing.

Written in 1989

By Vada Caldwell

God Speaks

I spoke to God and I heard Him say so clear
My precious child I will always be near.

Written in 1994

By Vada Caldwell

Yes Lord

Yes Lord, Yes
Thank you for happiness
For each touch and caress
Yes Lord, Yes.

Thank you for flowers that bloom
For the sun, stars and moon.
Thank you for quiet solace
As here I seek your face.

Touch my heart today, I pray
Guide me Lord, every step of the way.
In the quiet of my room
I travel to the empty tomb

And silently speak your name
As the gift of life I claim.
Yes Lord, Yes
Thank you for happiness.

Written by: Mrs. Vada Caldwell
May 13, 1995

Our Father

Holy are You!
Hallowed be your name
May your kingdom come in me.
You provide, I trust You,
Prayer is life.

God reaches out –
We have to reach out to Him!

Prayer is a full time relationship!
Praise your blessed and Holy Name.
Take my hand Dear God I pray.

Written by: Vada Caldwell
July 30, 1995

My Beloved One

Your strength shines through and is always there.
Willingly, your wisdom you constantly share.
You make our home a better place to live.
Your loving care and kindness you always give.

A good and faithful husband and companion to me.
For all to be able to know and see.
The gifts of the Spirit of God flourish and abide
within your heart.
All these you have given to me from the start.

A good father you have always been.
You've made our life one filled with joy.
Untold joy you bring to us day by day.
Your presence makes me happy in every way.

Written by:
Vada Caldwell

1996

Tommy & Vada
Caldwell

Tommy & Vada
Our Back Yard

God's Hand

There is a road we travel alone
Until for our sins we atone.
God's Hand reaches down from Heaven above
He whispers you are my child whom I love.

Trust in me, do not despair
You are my child, sheltered in my care.
My beloved Son intercedes for you.

Think and pray – soon you will see
My touch is here to heal,
From your sins you have been set free.

Written by
Vada Henson Caldwell - 1999

Life for Jesus

Life is filled with both joy and sorrow
Our God in Heaven planned it that way.
That's why we should not worry about tomorrow
Just live for Jesus every minute of every day!

Dear Lord, help me to always Praise your Name.
And hold out my hand as a friend
Seeking a soul for you to win.

Written by:
Vada Caldwell

1999

Sermons

Many sermons are never heard
Sermons are everywhere we look
Not just in the spoken word
But in God's Holy Book.

The message –
Free to all!
The blessed gift of Salvation!

Give me, Dear Lord, ears to hear and eyes to see.
Make me and mold me into what You would have me be.

Written by:

Vada Caldwell

2000

God Is in His Heaven

As I sat in my favorite chair in my special room and looked out the window this morning, my eyes almost missed the bright yellow bird sitting on a tree branch surrounded by the green leaves. One tiny bird brought me such joy and awe. As I watched, I almost held my breath hoping it would stay. He flew away and back again.

Then to my surprise and delight, a tiny, tiny chipmunk came to visit me. He walked up on the porch and peered at me thru the glass door.

Many different birds are all around eating at the feeders, squirrels busily jumping on the tree trunks are there too.

But the presence of the little yellow bird and the baby chipmunk gave me the greatest joy.

The sun becoming more and more bright bringing light into our world blessed my heart. God's beautiful creation in all its Glory brings peace to my soul.

Thank you, Dear Lord for this special place and this special time with you each day. Praise your Holy Name!

Written by:

Vada Caldwell

June 12, 2001

Good Morning Lord

Good Morning Lord, Here I am early in the morn
Ready to listen for your voice
As I sit here and pray
The daily chores and noise of the day
You have held at bay.
Thank you Lord for this glorious day.
In the early morning light
I find you in the peace and quiet.

Father God of all
I lift my heart to you
Thank you for your love,
Your grace and mercy.
Thank you for your beloved Son Jesus
And His love and sacrifice for me and all others.

Thank you Lord for my husband
And his love and faithfulness
Thank you Father for our children, grandchildren
and great grandchildren.
Bless each one of them thru out the day Dear Lord
Protect them from all harm.
Lead them and guide them in your way.
Keep them in your will.
Hold them close Dear Lord, I pray.

Send your angels to watch over them day and night.
Cindy, Ron, Ronnie, Johnny and Pam.
Stephen, Megan, Savannah and Nathaniel.
Tommy, Nancy, Sam, Craig, Lorrie Beth and Russell.
Cathy, Raymond, Amy, Becky and Jason.
These are my loved ones.

And my beloved husband I love him so much.
Bless him for all time I pray
Father for your touch.
Strengthen him and me spiritually, physically and mentally.
In Jesus Holy and precious name.

Written by: Mrs. Thomas H. Caldwell, Jr. (Vada) - May 12, 2001

Many Blessings Creating Blessed Memories

My husband Tommy and I spend most of our days just enjoying our time together and with the assurance of God's presence. We trust God and know that His all loving hands can and will take care of us.

We have a favorite room in our home with our favorite chairs. Tommy and our son built the room. The windows are all around and from floor to ceiling. We spend much of our time there. My favorite chair was my mother's. I begin my day in my chair with a cup of hot tea and my Bible. It is special to watch the day awake and the sun come shining through the trees. Most of our time at home is spent in this room.

One afternoon in April, Tommy quietly called to me, "Come here!" As I walked into the room he pointed outside. The most spectacular sight that I have ever seen was right there in our back yard. Every tree branch, every bird feeder, every inch of ground was covered with tiny bright yellow birds with black wings. It was awesome. I had never seen that many birds at one time anywhere. They were absolutely beautiful and shone like gold in the sunlight. You can only imagine the sound of these precious birds as they enjoyed themselves in our yard. They stayed for a long, long time and to our surprise and delight they were back the next day. Then the next day there were only a few, then even less came and now, often there is only one and sometimes as many as five. Tommy said they were on their way to another part of the country and rested from their journey for two days as our guests. Each time we see these little friends of ours, we are filled with joy and awe. I wish you could have seen them.

God has blessed us with a wonderful family and many friends and I thank Him for His goodness. I pray that each one of us will follow the guidance of our Father in Heaven and learn to walk in the continuing awareness that we are walking in the presence of God. May our Blessings abound making Precious Memories for our tomorrows.

By Vada Caldwell

July, 2001

Praise His Name

Praise His Name
He is always the same
He never fails
His love will prevail.

Come to me, Come to me.
He whispers each day
Praise His Name.

He my Shepherd will be
Bless me oh my Savior I pray.
Bless me my Savior I ask of Thee.

Praise His Name
He's always the same.

Written by: Vada Henson Caldwell - 2002

Come into My Heart

Blessed Jesus come into my heart and stay
Never from you let me stray.

Lord help me hold to your hand
And lead me Blessed Lord to the
Promised land.

Written by: Vada Henson Caldwell

December 1, 2002

Wednesday Afternoon, February 20, 2002
My Beloved Family and Friends,

I thank God daily for each of you and the part you have played in our lives. I decided I would write and share our experiences with you. I know so many of you have suffered sorrow and are experiencing illness in your own lives and through it all continue to trust in our God. I guess the main reason I wanted to write this letter is to share my love, my prayers and my faith.

Last year 2001, started out with very cold weather. We enjoyed special times with friends and family. Visited Maggie and Steve in March and August, they visited us in May. We ate at Miss Sipps numerous times and enjoyed delicious food. Cindy, Ron and Johnny came from Kentucky to visit, we went to Kentucky in May to celebrate the birthday of our great-granddaughter Savannah. Visited Aunt Mary Joe, Bertha, Dave and Anna. Went to Oklahoma to visit with friends Wally and Elaine Jones. The latter part of 2001 was filled with traumatic experiences. Our Thanksgiving and Christmas Holidays were different from ever before. Even so, we are blessed to have a loving God, wonderful friends and a caring and loving family.

In August we drove to Georgia to visit with my sister and family for a week. We had been there two days and received a call from home. Our youngest daughter Cathy was in the hospital, on oxygen and very ill. We hurriedly packed our things and set out for home. Cathy had been diagnosed with congestive heart failure and Grave's disease. She was in the hospital seven days then had to return for radioactive iodine treatments to "kill" the thyroid, and will have to take medication for the rest of her life. Her heart was so out of rhythm she had to have electrical shock treatments to shock her heart into rhythm. After this she did pretty well for a couple of months, then in October had to go back to the emergency room and it was discovered she had pulmonary hypertension.

When Tommy kissed me goodbye on the morning of October 24, 2001 as he left for a 9:30 appointment neither of us had any idea the trauma awaiting us before the end of the day. As he got out of his car to go into the office building he became very ill, a nurse walking by came to his aid. He told her our number and asked her to call me. He was vomiting and said he had a terrible headache. She helped him into the building and began to do all she could to make him comfortable, called me and said she had called an ambulance to take him to the hospital immediately. I told her to send him to Methodist Central and I would be right there. Tommy's brother, Don, came to get me and took me to the hospital. After a lot of waiting, praying and crying I was allowed to see Tommy and was told he must have immediate brain surgery to save his life. Doctor said he did not have time to wait around for me to sign permission papers, I told him to go. He said to me, "Say a prayer for your husband and while you are at it, say one for me too." They gave me very little hope for his recovery.

All the family arrived and we began our vigil in the Critical Care Waiting Room. After my call, Cindy and Ron rushed here from Kentucky to be by our side. So we were all together, supporting one another with love and prayers. After five hours of surgery the doctor came into the waiting room to talk to us. He said Tommy had come through the surgery just fine and that we would be able to see him in about another hour. He said to me, "Don't expect much response from him, he is critically ill and may not be able to speak or even indicate that he hears you when you speak to him," Huddled together, we all prayed and waited till we could see him. They called from the Trauma Critical Care Unit that we could come to see him.

God had performed a miracle! He knew us, knew who he was and was able to tell the doctor his name. So our days at Methodist Central Hospital began. Nancy, Tommy and I spent the night in the waiting room. During the weeks he spent in the Trauma Unit there were signs of encouragement each day; a squeeze of the hand, a wiggle of the toe, talking and calling us by name, speaking of going pheasant hunting, talking about his big truck that he called "Big Red". Slowly he improved, the day came I asked him if he knew who I was and he said yes. I asked him to tell me my name. He replied Vader Tater. Oh the joyous laughter that surrounded his bed in the corner of the Intensive Care Unit. Most of you know this was the name the children called me to make me angry when I was growing up.

Though we knew these accomplishments were only the beginning, we were filled with hope and praised God for his goodness. Family and friends throughout the country were praying for him continually.

There were many hurdles put in our way, from intensive care to a private room, was discovered his food was going into the lungs instead of his stomach. The alternative…implant a peg tube into his stomach through which he would be fed, this was done. From there he was sent to Health South Rehab Hospital. He was there two days and became gravely ill. I received a call in the middle of the night that they were taking him to the emergency room. My son and I traveled the lonely, dark road to the hospital with fear in our hearts. He was very, very sick. Constant vomiting and diarrhea for several days. It seemed the food they had been giving him was not being digested and was causing the vomiting and diarrhea. They experimented with various foods they could give him through the peg tube and found one that he could tolerate. So we thought our troubles were over.

A few days later his blood pressure dropped to 34 over 18; the nurse and I could not get any response from him. She called to the aid and said we have got to get him to the unit right away. They pushed him in his bed out of the room telling me they were taking him to unit. I asked them where and they replied we will come back for you. I stood in the middle of that empty hospital room crying and praying and wondering if I would ever see him alive again. I called Nancy and Cathy. The nurse came for me and took me to the Coronary Unit waiting room where I found Nancy and Cathy waiting. It was determined he had a very serious lung infection. So the vigil began again.

After days of treatment he was able to return to another private room and then back to the Rehab facility on December 7th. From there I brought him home on December 28th. They told me I would have a very difficult time taking care of him by myself and advised that I place him in a skilled care nursing home. After more days of tears and prayer, I was sure I could and would take care of him. After all God has blessed us with 55 years of marriage. Tommy was my protector, my rock, my love and my life. The morning of December 29th, I was exhausted after a sleepless night. Each day and each night was different from any we had experienced before. I lay by his side each night with his pajama top held tightly in my hand to prevent him from getting out of bed and falling.

On December 29th our daughter Cathy was attacked by a dog and bitten in the face on each side of her mouth. She was rushed to emergency room where a plastic surgeon operated on her with more than 40 stitches in her precious face. When she got home, she told her husband Raymond that she was going to bed, cover her head and not come out again until 2002. Which she just about had to do because of shock, pain and a weakened body.

On January 10, 2002 Tommy and I were both feeling poorly. As we sat in our chairs, he suddenly told me, "I cannot breathe and my chest hurts, please call 911". I called and the ambulance came and took us to the hospital. While standing beside Tommy's bed in the emergency room, I became ill. They checked me over and admitted me to the emergency room in the same room with him. My heart was racing so fast it seemed it was trying to beat its way out of my chest. My blood pressure was 164 over 106. Tommy and I both were admitted to the hospital. He was on the 7th floor and I was on the 5th.

Monday, January 14, 2002 we each had a heart catherization. Tommy had blockage which will be treated with medication. I had blockage and heart rate out of rhythm. I had a pacemaker put in on January 15 and am taking medication. I was released from the hospital on January 17th and the nurse took me in a wheel chair to Tommy's room to kiss him goodbye. It was a sad goodbye for me and for him.

The decision is no longer mine, I am physically unable to take care of my beloved. He was released from the hospital on January 30th and moved to a skilled care nursing home. A wonderful minister friend of ours said to me, "I know you want to take care of him, but the very best care you can give him is by placing him in a skilled care home". Tommy walks with assistance, speaks well and knows each of us. I believe with all my heart they will help him and someday he will be able to come home. This is my constant prayer.

One night in Tommy's hospital room, I picked up the Bible and began to turn the pages. I came to Psalm 91, Verse 2 reads...I will say of the Lord, He is my refuge and my fortress: my God; in him will I trust. Verse 11 reads...For he shall give his angels charge over thee, to keep thee in all thy ways. All of this Psalm speaks to my heart and gives me great comfort. Truly, I do trust in God and His love, mercy and grace. May he strengthen each of us spiritually, mentally and physically each day is my prayer for you, your family, me and my family.

With a burdened and grateful heart I thank him every day for all his blessings.

God is good and merciful.

Please continue to pray for us and I will continue to pray for each of you.

With much love,

Vada, 2002

As Paul Harvey used to say: Now for the rest of the story.

The next day when I arrived at the (Skilled) Nursing Home I found my husband on a mattress on the floor. The nurse explained to me the reason for this treatment was they were afraid he would fall out of the bed. I felt this was a bit bizarre but went along with it.

They were to give him speech and physical therapy. Each day I asked to see and speak to the therapist, I was always told they were not available at that time. Most of the time when I arrived he was wet and his bed was wet. This continued. I never saw a therapist or doctor.

After 30 days, the nurse told me they were going to move him to the regular nursing area as Medicare would no longer pay for skilled care. This was a step down as far as care was concerned. I told her to forget it that I was taking him home, which I did. I knew with God's help I could take better care of him. He had spent thirty days of neglect and absolutely no skilled care.

My precious Tommy was so happy to get home, he almost ran to his chair, and he really could not walk, but our Lord helped him. I hired a helper to come to the house and give him his bath and various ways of helping him. It took three or four women before we found an angel named Bessie. She worked three days a week and was so kind, loving and compassionate not to mention the outstanding care she gave. Very soon she became like one of our family and worked for us seven and one half years, a true gift from God.

Tommy and I continued daily to be thankful for our family and the love we shared. We celebrated our 59th Wedding Anniversary on June 15, 2005. Even though we experienced illness and difficult times we never failed to Praise God for His Blessings. We had our daily Bible reading and prayer. Every evening he would call me and say, "Read the Bible." I spent most of the afternoon with him beside his bed.Sometimes when I was in the other part of the house he would call me, I would go to him and ask, What is it honey? He would say, I just need you. He was bedridden, and it was my privilege to care for him.

On March 1, 2005 serious illness came my way and on May 10, I had double major surgery. I was in the hospital 23 days and then several months of recovery. During all these months our three children; Cindy, Tommy and Cathy took care of their Dad and me. Even though they each have their own family and work responsibility, they scheduled their time so each of them could alternate coming to care for us. Bessie still came three days a week. What a tremendous blessing for Tommy and me. I can never praise them and their families enough for all they have done and continue to do. I thank God for all of them.

Our lives were truly filled with God's blessings, love and happiness. Our children have always loved me and their Dad and had the utmost respect for him during his life. He was the best husband and father anyone could have. And now, I must share the testimony of our baby girl Cathy of her love for her Daddy written to him in 2008.

Things I Learned from My Dad

I was reading the paper on Father's Day, 2008, and there were several letters from people telling about the things they learned from their Fathers. It got me to thinking about my father. The first thing that came to my mind made me laugh, because, you see, my father taught me how to clean the bathtub. My Mom worked days and my Dad worked nights, so he was with my brother, sister and me during the day. He taught us to clean the house for Mom. My job was the bathroom. And I tell you to this day I can clean a bathroom so good, it looks like a picture from a magazine.

Of course he taught me other things like how to drive and things of that nature, but the most important things I learned from my Dad were "life lessons."

My father taught me compassion, kindness, humility, decency, and love. I could go on and on but I think you understand what I'm trying to convey. My father to me is a giant among men. He is strong, intelligent, kind-hearted, compassionate, and especially loving. The only time I ever saw him really angry was when some injustice had been done, either to a family member or stranger. So, yes I learned from my father that prejudice and injustices were wrong.

Let me share with you the most poignant lesson I learned from my father. I learned love. My father loves his family so much it always seems to glow from his being. He also loves the "Lord" with all his heart and of course, this was passed down to his children.

Now he is stricken down with illness, to me he is still a giant among men. Even though he can't speak very well now, I get the feeling he's trying to teach me one more lesson. That lesson is to love and honor Mama, because he loves her so much that when he leaves us he wants to make sure that Mama is going to be taken good care of. And, I promise you Daddy, that she will be.

Happy Father's Day Daddy! I love you.

Mary Catherine Caldwell Farr

Cathy kept her promise. Her Daddy died in March of 2009. Cathy died from a heart attack in 2012.

With much sorrow, I miss the two of them every day.

They will never be forgotten. They were both very special!

Vada and Tommy Caldwell, Christmas 2006

Jesus the Son

To know Jesus the Son
Is to know God the Father.
God loved us so much that He gave His Son
Jesus loved us so much that He gave Himself.

In Jesus we find rest for our souls.
Spiritual rest is strength in Jesus,
Our Lord, our Savior and Redeemer.

Come unto me says Jesus –
And we who believe –
Come for worship
Love – guidance
Grace – mercy – strength
and
Life everlasting.

By: Vada Caldwell - 2002

Recently as the day began to awake, I spent my early morning quiet time in my favorite room sitting in my favorite chair. I looked down into the woods at all the different trees and my special one just outside the window. God spoke to me with these words.

Daybreak

If trees could talk I wonder what they would say.
Look at me, I am tall, straight, a majestic sight.
I am short, crooked and bent perhaps the most pitiful sight of all.
Oh, I don't know - look at me; most of my bark is missing.
All my leaves are gone – Mine is a sorrowful plight.
Hey, I am very old, once very tall, but now I am bent low.
In searching for the sunlight to help me grow I turned this way and that.

My roots are deep and strong; I have weathered many a storm.
My trunk is covered with many branches, some have been injured and
broken, yet they hold tight to me.
The storms have come and gone and I still stand.
God made me strong enough to bend with the wind.

My friends are all different you see -
For that is the way God meant it to be.
So come and grow old with me.
Let us travel the road together
In fair or stormy weather.

We human beings could learn much about life as we watch
and listen to each and every tree.

My friends, we are all different you see -
For that is the way God meant it to be.
So come and grow old with me.

In fair or stormy weather.
Let us travel the road together.

Written by: (Vada)

Mrs. Thomas H. Caldwell, Jr.

Merry Christmas to One and All

This holiday season may your days be merry and bright!

AS THIS YEAR TRAVELS OUT OF SIGHT
WE BID OUR GOODBYE TO THE OLD
AND UNWRAP OUR GIFT OF A NEW YEAR
OUR THOUGHTS WILL ECHO A CHEER,
PERHAPS FOLLOWED BY THE SHEDDING 0F A TEAR.

MAY ALL OUR DAYS BE FILLED WITH GOLD.
THE GOLD OF FRIENDSHIP, LOVE AND GOOD HEALTH
THIS IS TRULY THE BLESSING OF UNTOLD WEALTH!

From Tom and Vada

December 2, 2002

My Wish for You and Me

I wish for us ....

God's comfort on difficult days,
Hugs and kisses to strengthen our spirits
Smiles and laughter when sadness betrays.
Rainbows and sunsets to warm our souls.

God's love ever present to encourage and console.
His beauty everywhere we look
Courage to know and accept ourselves as God made us
According to His Holy Book.

Friendships to brighten our way.
Confidence when we doubt
Faith so we will continue to believe,
Patience to accept the truth,
And love to complete our lives day by day.

May our Father in Heaven lead, guide. guard and direct us I pray!

Written by: Mrs. Thomas H. Caldwell, Jr. (Vada) - Year 2003

Speak to Me

Speak to me oh God in the early morning light
Make all my worries and tribulations take flight.
Thank you God for this day you have made.
Filled with love, sunshine and shade.

I love you my Precious Lord.
I seek shelter in the shade of your love
As you have promised in your Word
Your blessings will flow from Heaven above.

Written By: Vada Caldwell

January 2003

This Is Me

Vada Henson Caldwell

Wife of One
Mother of three
Grandmother of eight
Mother-in- Law of three
Great Grandmother of eight
Grandmother-in-Law of three
What a wonderful family God has given to me.

May I always bring Joy
Into their hearts.
It is my prayer that they will feel my love
Every day and in every way!

Written by Vada Henson Caldwell – April 25, 2003

A Picture of Grace and Beauty

The flowers are blooming, the trees are budding and
becoming fully clothed every day.

The dogwoods are filled with blooms throughout the woods
In the valley below our home.

The buttercups in my yard have lifted their heads and brought
me much joy.

What a gloriously beautiful sight!

May each of us find joy as we view God's beauty around us.

Words of Thought
Vada Caldwell
April 6, 2003

God's World

Tis very clear to see
God made this world for you and me.

If we could but fully understand
His great and divine plan.

How great it would be to live in this great land
In harmony and peace

Among every child, woman and man.

By: Vada Caldwell

May 19, 2003

Majestic Creation

Tis strange the beauty that meets the eye
From up above the earth so high
It is sure the Master's Hand did plan
That which we see as far as the eye can span.

Surely if an atheist ever flew on a plane
He could not help but happily exclaim
None other than the Almighty God supreme
Could make the world below into such a Majestic theme!

By: Vada Caldwell - 2003

His Hand Is with Me!

As I trod the road of life here on earth
I thank you God for Jesus' birth.

I have so much for which to Thank You!
The wonderful peace I feel today
In this room with your presence so near
This time of watching the day awake
I feel so blessed as I sit here and pray.

Bless my Tommy today Lord
Strengthen him physically, mentally and spiritually.
And I could use some strength too!

My blessed Lord so dear,
As *Jabez prayed so long ago
I lift up my voice to you
Bless me today Dear God, enlarge my territory.
May your hand be with me.
Keep me from evil
That I may cause no pain.

Blessed Savior hear my plea
As I pray on bended knee
Grant our wish Lord for Tommy to eat.
Let your miracle of healing be complete.
And we will thank you and praise your Holy Name,
And to you be all Honor, Glory and Praise!

Mrs. Vada Caldwell

October, 2003

*Prayer of Jabez

I Chronicles Chapter 4, vs. 9-10

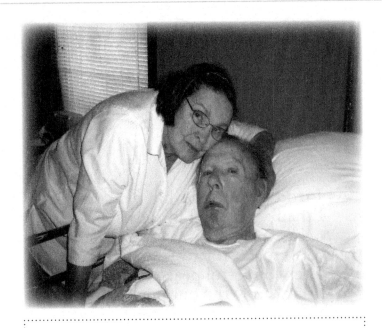

Vada and Tom

Our children, Cathy, Cindy & Tommy
with their Dad Christmas 2006

How Is Tom?

He is held up by my prayers every day
I greet him each morning.
I say "Good morning darling, I love you.
He searches my face as he looks into my eyes
And he always, always replies
And I love you too!

Every day I thank God for this man of mine.
And for the years we have had filled with happiness sublime.

How is Tom?
He is often in pain, nauseated and weak.
Our days often are spent in pain and fear.
I wonder and pray Dear Lord, as your answer I seek.
What is to become of the one I hold so dear?

He is my life, my love, my all
My husband so handsome and tall.

For these many years he has cared
for me as I leaned on him
Now it is my privilege and joy
To hold him and let him lean on me.

I love him so and I know Dear God you
love him too.
Our gracious God we place ourselves in
your hand.
We trust in you and your loving plan.
For you have always been true.

Written by:
Vada Caldwell 2004

The Bible Says

EPHESIANS   Chapter One Vs 3

"Blessed be the God and Father of our Lord Jesus Christ, who hath blessed us with all spiritual blessings in heavenly places in Christ."

HEAVENLY PLACES
IS ANYWHERE THAT I ALLOW MYSELF THE
JOY AND PEACE OF BEING STILL TO FEEL AND ACKNOWLEDGE
THE BLESSED PRESENCE OF JESUS IN MY LIFE.

WHERE HE IS:
IT IS HEAVENLY.

EPHESIANS 2 Vs. 10

"For we are his workmanship, created in Christ Jesus unto good works, which God hath before ordained that we should walk in them."

FAITH IN GOD WILL HELP US IN ALL THAT WE DO. WHEN WE WALK WITH CHRIST WE ARE SAFE AND OUR FAITH TELLS US THAT GOD'S ETERNAL PURPOSE WILL BE TRIUMPHANT.

From the heart of
Vada Caldwell

The Mystery

Something happens to the heart in December. Something starts singing in the soul. All the earth seems to feel the mystery of a glorious event.

Matthew 2:1-2 Now when Jesus was born in Bethlehem of Judea in the days of Herod the king, behold, there came wise men from the east to Jerusalem, saying, where is he that is born King of the Jews? For we have seen his star in the east, and are come to worship him.

The Christmas road leads to an inn. It is the inn of our lives. It may be today, as two thousand years ago, that the rooms are filled. In one room we find self-interest, in another pleasure, in another indifference and so on. Our inn of many rooms may not have room for our love of Christ. If we will clear the rubbish from our best room, He will come in and we will find we are living in a new world, a world where love rules and bitterness and strife are not known.

Come into our hearts, Lord Jesus. May we have thankful hearts for Thee, but quiet homes of prayer and praise, where needful cares of life are wisely ordered and put away. Where wide spaces are kept for Thee and holy thoughts are all around.

When the Christmas candles are burned out; the carols have died away; the star is set and the wonderful, thrilling song of the night is past, you Lord God remain with us and fill us with the Joy and Blessedness of Thy Glorious Birth.

From the depths of our hearts we repent of our sins and humbly ask for your forgiveness. May we always seek your will for our lives and be ever thankful for your Salvation free to all.

Like the wise men of old, we press forward with our eyes fixed upon the Star, seeking the Christ Child, the Savior of the world.

Vada Caldwell

Be Not Afraid

Oh Dear God, I was sore afraid
Then I found written in your word
"Whosoever will".

How my heart swelled with joy
When your voice came to me so clear
Be not afraid child of mine
I have been there all the time.

I tried to tell you when you called in prayer
The way to grow in Spirit is to share
Your love for Jesus, your blessed Lord.
You just locked the door and hid me within.

Show me to others from day to day
Live for me and continue to pray.
Be assured I died for your sins to atone
Call unto me, you are never alone.

Written by:
Vada Caldwell
May, 2004

My Heart - My Life

I gave my heart to Jesus
At the tender age of ten.
I vowed from that day forward
To live a life free from sin.

This I tried to do in my own power
Every minute of every day, hour by hour.
But that is not the way,
I heard my Savior say.
A baby needs food to live by
And so do you my little one.

I failed oh so many times
I knew I loved my Jesus
And I hoped He loved me too.
My child you invited me in
Don't you know I've always been by your side?

I feared my sins were not forgiven
And really didn't know if I would make it
to heaven.
Lord, did you really die for me?

When I invited my Savior in, I locked him tightly inside
As though He was something to hide.
But oh my precious Lord kept tugging at my heart
Saying, my beloved child, Believe!
For with you I will abide.

Written by:

Vada Caldwell

Come Closer

We have just celebrated Holy Week and experienced the joy of Easter. I am reminded of a trip my husband Tommy and I took to Brazil in 1970.

One day our guide drove us along winding roads through the jungle and up the mountain. When we reached the mountain top, we came upon this incredibly huge marble statue of Christ with outstretched arms. We were drawn to this magnificent statue that seemed to be inviting us to Come Closer. As we drew closer and knelt at his feet we could see his face more clearly. This day gave us a blessed memory.

Years later I read about a man who visited a statue of Christ and was disappointed in what he saw until a little child took him by the hand and said, "Come Closer and kneel." As he let the little child lead him and knelt, his heart was thrilled.

Today our Christ stands with outstretched arms and invites us "Come unto me."
As we accept His invitation, let us
Come Closer, Kneel and Seek His Face.

In Christian Love,

Vada Caldwell

Written for:

Our Church Newsletter

March 2005

Sorrow and Joy

Experiencing sorrow, brings memories of joy. Maybe God prepared our hearts this way.

Embury church graveyard is holy ground and filled with faithful children of God. Two of them are my husband Thomas Caldwell and our daughter-in-law Nancy Caldwell.

Tommy was an honorable man, a wonderful loving husband, father grandfather and great-grandfather. He was proud of his family and showed his love in words and actions. He was not ashamed to shed tears of sadness and happiness. He loved and honored his mother and father and was a loving and respectful son. I could say so many things about him and his character, he never used foul language, he was honest and trustworthy, and ready to lend a helping hand to others. Most importantly, my husband loved God and Embury church.

Although he was bedridden for the last seven and one half years of his life, he continued to pray for our family and our church. He served God and the church faithfully all the days of his life. He cared for his family, laughed and wept with and for all of us day by day.

Our daughter-in-law Nancy was special. She was a loving and thoughtful wife, mother, daughter, and sister. She quietly helped others. She loved and served God faithfully. She spoke with kindness, was thoughtful and filled with grace. Tommy and I loved her very much and she loved us. We could not have asked for a better daughter-in-law, she was more like a daughter to us. As Tommy lay in his bed and she was so very ill, every day he would ask about her and we would say our prayers. When she died it was a rough time for us. Our hearts were broken and we cried together.

Nancy served our Church for many years as Secretary of Church Council. She taught the young people in Sunday School many years. I know without a doubt she left an impression upon them they will always remember.

Tommy and Nancy will never be forgotten. When I think of them I am reminded of the scripture, "Blessed are the pure in heart for they shall see God".

They were pure in heart.

Written by: Vada Caldwell 2009

133

My Daughter-
In-Law Nancy

My Husband Tommy

Lorrie Beth, My Son Tommy,
Sam, Russell & Nancy

The Glorious Sunrise

Today as my eyes viewed the majesty of God's world
My thoughts turned to the winter days of not so long ago.
As day by day the north winds continued to blow.
When the ground was covered with a blanket of snow.
The flowers deep beneath the blanket of earth no longer
could grow.

This morning as I looked into the beauty of God's skies
My soul drank in the glorious sunrise.
I began to realize how so wonderful is His great and
majestic plan.
The flowers are blooming and the trees are dressed again.

Praise God for His loving kindness and enduring love for His
people all over our land.

From the heart of
Vada Henson Caldwell

2016

The Creation of Seasons

God in his creation of the tree
Reveals to you and to me
His glorious and wonderful plan
For the seasons of life for beast and man.

In the cold, cold months the barren trees all
grope for the sky.
Spring appears and God says, "Here am I".
The clothing of earth is re-arranged
With the touch of God's hand, the season is changed.

Once again trees are covered with leaves, and the birds
begin to sing.
Through the forest glades, rays of sunshine radiantly beam.
Creating a haven of refuge for God's animals to thrive.
The wonder of creation exclaims, He is Alive!

Written by:
Vada Caldwell

A Song in My Heart

The warmth of my blanket
around my shoulders
And
The warmth of God
in my heart
Fills
My life with joy and peace
And
Puts a song in my heart and soul.

By: Vada Caldwell

June 26, 2012

He Is the One

Only God can set us free
He is the one who holds the key.
He gave His Son for you and me.

If we come to Him on bended knee
He will hear our every plea.
And will whisper, "My child,
Come unto me."

Written by: Vada Caldwell

May 21, 2016

My Love

The love I have for you dear one
Shall never depart from thee.
The greatest love under the sun
Greater than a sailor's love for the sea.

When I think of you my dear
It is a feeling of love, respect and tenderness.
And usually I shed a few tears
And wish you were here with me.

My love for thee dear one
Shall always live within me
There will be none greater under the sun.
I declare my love will ever be.

Vada Caldwell

Our Gracious Heavenly Father

My dearest Lord, my gracious Heavenly Father I come to you in prayer. I thank you for your love, your grace and your mercy and for all the many blessings you have showered upon me and my family and friends all the days of our lives.

Forgive us Lord for our sins. Lead us in your way and keep us in your will. Let us be reminded again and again that the apostle Paul said, "I glory in nothing but Christ crucified, as the salvation of my soul."

Father let us always remember this and be aware we must not glory in our worldly privileges, our own works, our own knowledge or our own graces. Forbid that we should glory save in the Cross of our Lord Jesus Christ. Keep us ever mindful, that the Cross is the strength of each of us, the secret of our prosperity, our success and the salvation of our souls.

It is with humble and grateful hearts that we ask your blessings and your protection from harm. Be with us every day and night Father that we may always glorify your precious name and live in a way that will always be pleasing to you.

In the name of our Lord, Jesus Christ we pray, thy will be done.
Amen

Vada Caldwell

June 11, 2016

God's Blessings Over and Over

As I looked out the window this morning a tiny, colorful hummingbird came to the bird feeder looking for food. He flew from place to place and did not find anything to eat. Every year they have come to this yard and found food. Feeders need to be bought, filled and hung for these precious little ones.

Tommy and I have repeatedly been blessed by their visits since he and Tommy Son built our room onto the house. Now we cannot sit together and share our awe and excitement over our little feathered friends. Since Tommy's stroke in 2001 he is unable to walk, and is bedridden. We are blessed and thankful the stroke did not affect his mind or speech. We spend a lot of time sharing our life. I read the Bible to him every day. When I have someone to come and get him out of bed into the wheelchair, then we can take him to the living room.

Our room is a special place where we spent our time together enjoying watching birds and animals and seeing all the trees. The room is inaccessible to the wheelchair so we miss that special joy. God is good. He has blessed us and continues to bless us every day.

YEARS HAVE PASSED. My beloved left this world for a better place in March, 2009. It is now Wednesday morning, June 29, 2016 at 5:30am. I awoke at 3:30am and could not go back to sleep so I got up. I have been typing poems to put into a book for publication and came across a slip of paper on which I had written the above in 2003 and decided to put it in my book. God continues to bless me but my life without my precious husband is quite different.

My beloved daughter Mary Catherine died in the year 2012 and is buried beside her Daddy and then the horrible disease cancer took my precious granddaughter Lorrie Beth at the age of 35 in 2014 and she is buried beside her mother Nancy who died in 2007 from cancer.

So the Embury Cemetery is the resting place for my family. A row of graves Mary Catherine, My husband Tommy, Nancy and Lorrie Beth side by side.

My son Tommy lives next door with his wife Tammie. They are blessed and spend a lot of time with me and with his grandson A.J., Lorrie Beth's son, and all the other grandchildren.

My daughter Cindy and her husband Ron live with me in my home. We have a good life together. They help me and I help them. We enjoy a lot of time spent with their grandchildren, my great grandchildren.

God blesses and cares for all of us. I am so wealthy and tremendously blessed. Thank you Dear God in Jesus Name.

Mrs. Thomas H. Caldwell, Jr. (Vada Henson)

June 29, 2016

6:00am

72 Degrees

Sweet Baby Jesus Boy

Baby Jesus in swaddling clothes
Laughing eyes and smiling face
And ten little toes.

One so small
answering his Father's call
will give His all
for those who seek him.

Amazing Grace!

Written by: Vada Caldwell

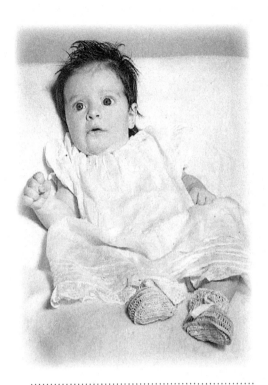

Baby Cindy 1948

Cindy – High School

Cindy – College Graduate

Our Firstborn Child

To Cindy, Our blessing from God.
So precious and beautiful at your birth
A jewel of great worth.
I pray that all the days to come
Will bring you joy and happiness one by one.

As you travel the road of life
Go forth our precious love
With guidance from above.
Life is filled with promises bright
As daily you walk in God's light.

In you, God has given us a special gift,
And we thank Him every day.
Our precious daughter, we love you so,
To what extent you will never know.

So much joy and happiness you have brought our way.
As we watched you grow day by day.
Each day and milestone life to you imparts
Is one more treasure to hide in our hearts.

Written by: Your Mother Vada Caldwell

Added this Sunday afternoon, July 3, 2016.

My life is filled with great joy
With your presence day by day.
Since your Daddy's death I have been sad
But the times you and I enjoy together
Have made me not as sad but glad.
I thank my God above
For you my daughter and your love!

Cynthia Anne Caldwell

August 24, 1948

Ron and Cindy Pritchard in Hot Springs

Ron and Cindy

Very few people really know
All the happiness a child will show
Down the years you will wonders see
And be thankful as you hold yours on your knee.

Could you but slightly guess
All the joys your life will possess.
Love as you have never known
Dear little babies bring to a home.

My prayer for you, your little girl or boy
Each day as you pass thru this world of ours
Love, happiness, pride and joy
Lingering throughout life
As your child makes the years seem like hours.

A blessing our great God to you will impart
A precious child to hold and love.
I pray with all my heart
The three of you will trust in our Lord above.

Train up a child in the way he should go
The bible says this you know.
So love your child with all your body, mind and soul
And you will find your life to be complete and whole.

Written by:

Vada Caldwell

November, 1970

Ron and Cindy

Their three Children,
Pam, Ronnie & Johnny

This Is the Day

Truly this is the day the Lord hath made and I will rejoice
and be glad in it.

With the help of God, I will move forward and onward day by
day in this New Year of 1979. Thank you Dear Lord for the
blessings you have given me and mine in such abundance
throughout all the days of my life. Continue to lead us dear Lord
in your ways and keep us in your will, for it is in the name of
Jesus that I pray.

Heavenly Father you and I know my wrongs and things I
need to change in my life. Touch my heart Father and cleanse
my soul of each dark blot. Lead me the way you would have me go.

Bless my loved ones Lord. Bless the poor, sick and
afflicted. Bless the members of my family and church Father.
I could call the name of many in need of prayer dear Lord, but
you know who they are before I speak.

Bless everybody, everywhere Lord, one and all for it is in
the name of Jesus, thy beloved Son that I pray.

Vada Caldwell

January, 1979

Early Morning Hours

Oh God I Pray, Help Me, Help Me Today!

Psalm 91 Vs. 1:

He that dwelleth in the secret place of the most high God shall abide under the shadow of the Almighty. Vs. 11: For he shall give his angels charge over thee, to keep thee in all thy ways.

What a Wonderful Promise. Lord may I always abide in the heart of the most high God and keep you in my heart.

February 1, 1991- 3:30 am

As I dressed, the words, "I will seek thy face early in the morning" came to mind. I went to my studio and reached for my Bible and opened it and the scripture Mark 1:35 appeared and was underlined. It read – And in the morning, rising up a great while before day, he went out, and departed into a solitary place, and there he prayed. A message to me? I think so. I bowed my head and prayed. Then I continued to read. Turning the pages again and again my eyes came to rest on Ephesians 2:8 and on thru 3rd and 4th chapters. God's Word speaks to us when we listen.

Mark 4: 30, 31, & 32

Whereunto shall we liken the kingdom of God? Or with what comparison shall we compare it? It is like a grain of mustard seed, which when it is sown in the earth, is less than all the seeds that be in the earth:But when it is sown, it grows up, and becomes greater than all herbs, and shoots out great branches; so that the fowls of the air may lodge under the shade of it.

Psalm 31 Vs 24

Be of good courage, and He shall strengthen your heart, all ye that hope in the Lord.

Vada Caldwell - August 8, 2016

God Reveals Himself

God reveals himself to us in many different ways. He invites us to reveal our hearts to Him each and every day.

In the scripture of John 3:16 we read, "For God so loved the world that he gave His only begotten Son that whosoever believeth in Him should not perish but have Everlasting Life. In the book of Genesis, God speaks and the world comes into existence. A world created by God filled with the redeeming love of God.

God reveals himself to man both in the Old and New Testaments. In the Old Testament God called Moses to deliver the Israelites from bondage and declared them to be His chosen people even though the Bible states they did not even know His Name. God's Grace has always been given freely. He has always come to us in love and with open arms. We find both redemption and reconciliation to God through Christ and His undying love. We are taught the conditions of our earthly birth are unimportant. The important thing is our relationship to God – both now and forever. All who are willing to accept the Son of God and believe in Him will become children of God. Only Christ was born the Son of God.

We become sons simply by believing in Christ! By His redeeming grace we are saved. We find God when we let go and give in to the simple truth that:

GOD IS!

The Word was God. The Word is God.

God was, God is, and God will be forever!

Our Commitment to God places us in a Special Relationship to God. True commitment is much more than just keeping the rules of life and worship. It is a matter of our offering to God - - all that we are, all that we have and all that we hope to be. Full consecration of ourselves to God is the reason for our existence.

We were made: By God for God!

Vada Henson Caldwell

God's Only Begotten Son

Jesus a tiny baby boy born to Save the World.
A babe in swaddling clothes to bring blessings to all who
would receive Him.
He grew into a young boy nurtured and loved. As he questioned his
elders they were astounded by his spiritual knowledge.

God's only begotten Son was born, lived, died, buried and rose
again. He bore the sins of you and me so we could become children of
God and be given Eternal Life.

Praise be to God.

Written by:

Vada Caldwell

December 31, 1986

The Strength of the Christian Life

Ropes are made from sisal fiber, which comes from all parts of the world. They are made into bales and fed into machines, fast and slow and then treated with an oil solution. As they are put through several processes together, they become stronger and stronger. Eventually they are made into ropes too strong for human hands to break. We could compare this to the Christian life.

The many strands of fiber are the church members. Individually they are simple to break. Add a little oil (church fellowship) which brings the members together more and more. Through their being together they learn more about one another, begin working together as the children of their Father in Heaven. After more and more fellowship, we begin to pray together and realize the strength and joy we share and the wonderful opportunity offered us in living the Christian life. Like the rope, we have been directed along the true path of faith, hope and love which strengthens more and more each time we meet together.

Now even the rope in its finished state has a breaking point just as we individually can find ourselves in the same condition. If we place too much stress and strain on the individual without showing them that God is there to share their burden then they might stretch and finally break.

If we work together we strengthen one another. We always need strength from drawing together to learn God's Word. In lifting a helping hand to others, we are also lifting a helping hand to ourselves.

Yet another way to strengthen ourselves is to realize and share the knowledge that God is with us always. He is with us ALWAYS and we are CALLED to be HIS LIGHT in HIS WORLD.

Written by:

Vada Henson Caldwell

On Mother's Day in the Church Bulletin

My Mother spent her life giving to her family and others.
She had a deep and abiding faith in her God, and believed in the
power of prayer. She taught me the difference between good and
bad, the importance of others, and all about the love of God.
She laughed with me, and cried with me. She held me in her arms and
kissed my hurt away. The memory of her touch burns deep within my
soul. I miss her very much. I thank God for my Mother, and wish I
could take her hand in mine and say, "Mama, I love you!"

My Mother Annie Wilma Yopp Henson

Vada Caldwell

On Father's Day in the Church Bulletin

My Daddy died when I was 18 years old. My memories of his love and
life are many, but my fondest memory of my Father is my hand in his
as we walked through the woods, his arms around me as all my hurts
he understood, and his beautiful clear tenor voice as he sang of God's
Amazing Grace . . .I loved him so very much and oh I miss him so.

My Daddy L. D. Henson

Vada Caldwell

God in Heaven

Each morning when I first awake, Dear God I come to you
I pray in the name of Jesus, your blessed Son.
I pray Dear God in heaven for your healing touch
Upon my husband, I love him so much.
I thank you for hearing my plea as I pray each one by one
And thank you for answering too.

I place my trust in your blessed hand
For I know you will hear and understand.
In the Name of my Lord and Savior,
I pray Father Thy Will Be Done.

Written by: Vada Caldwell

A Man

Today I met a man with tear-dimmed eyes
He took me by the hand
And with words so wondrous wise
Told me how God had blessed his life
Thru years of joy intermingled with strife.

I listened to a man speak today
Whose outward skin was black
When he began to pray
It was evident our hearts and minds were on the same
track.

Today our paths have met
Truly a blessing I'll never forget.
Today I touched a man's skin
And something happened to my heart within.

This man became my friend
We shared the thoughts in our heart
It mattered not the color of our skin.

We prayed, God bless this world of ours
Fill each of us with love divine
So that in our waking hours,
Our lives for You will shine.

Thank you Lord for your touch
Upon all the many children of yours
Whose lives with your love brightly shine
And want all to know they are truly thine
As they joyfully await their home with You
in Heaven above.

Vada Caldwell

One Yellow Rose

The young man and woman sat beneath the stars at a sidewalk café. The night was beautiful, a short rain had just freshened the air. They could hear the sound of the waves of the Atlantic washing upon the Copacabana Beach of Rio. Lovers strolled along the beach. The night was cool and restful with a sprinkling of stars in the sky.

A small boy came walking by with a bunch of roses in his hand. The roses were slightly crushed and wilted. The boy asked the man, do you want to buy a rose. Just one cruizero he said, just one rose for the lady?

When the young man bought the rose, the boy ran away with glee. I am sure he felt he had made a tremendous sale and maybe even laughed at the American. But what the boy did not know was that five or even ten cruizero's would not have been too much. The husband had purchased a token of love for his wife. One single yellow rose to have and to hold with joy!

Mrs. Vada Caldwell

Dr. J. Hays Brantley 2016

My Doctor

Doctors study and struggle for many years
Through long hours of hard work and even some tears
To reach the goal they strive to attain
And pledge their lives to end suffering and pain.

Some quickly forget their Hippocratic Oath
Thinking only of their clientel's growth
And how to glorify their name
By making a place in the hall of fame.

We know the world is a busy place
Still we are all individuals of the human race
So thank God there are doctors who care
And take time to listen and your burdens to share.

I'd rather know one doctor with love in his heart
Than ten whose self-sought fame has set them apart.

My doctor hung his shingle on the door
Saying, come to me and suffer no more.
And people keep coming by the score
They need his assurance that comes oe'r and oe'r.

The doctor I speak of stands out from all the rest
For with a tender heart he has truly been blessed.
My doctor, I'd like the world to know,
His name is J. Hays Brantley and I love him so.

Written by: Vada H. Caldwell

April 26, 2016

Our Mighty and Most High God

This morning September 2, 2016 during my Quiet Time, my eyes came to rest on the scripture Zephaniah 3:17. I had highlighted this verse sometime in the past.

It reads: The Lord thy God in the midst of thee is mighty; he will save, he will rejoice over thee with joy; he will rest in his love, he will joy over thee with singing.

I thought my goodness, what a wonderful promise. What a marvelous revelation to me.

My God is singing to me.
He is singing to me!

Oh my great God Jehovah I hear your voice as you sing to me.

My blessed Father God, to you I lift my voice in song.
I love you Dear God, please keep me from all wrong.
Lead me my precious Lord in my walk with thee.
For with you and in your holy presence I belong.

Written by:

Vada Caldwell

September 2, 2016

This I Pray

Jesus Precious Lord, listen as I pray
Gracious one, hear our prayer this day.

Keep our thoughts and actions
far beyond reproach.
So others might see us as Christian folks.

There is a whisper in my heart
That your holy presence will impart
Thy love and joy into every new morning.
As we view the glory of each dawning.

Thank you blessed Father for your touch and
loving Spirit to guide us.
In Jesus precious and holy Name
All honor, praise and glory be thine!

Written by:

Vada Caldwell

August 25, 2016

Love One Another

God's highest goal for us as Christians is "To love one another." Christians have trials, tribulations and Joy. The joy of a Christian is given to us by the loving Spirit of God. If we want to enjoy the Christian life, we will love others, not only those who love us but the unlovable as well.

Jesus wants us to love one another. He loves all of us. He looks inside the vessel and sees the inner man and fills him with his Spirit of Love. The Joy of a Christian is Love . . . for one another.

Nothing in life is more important than God's highest purpose for His children. God's Word declares that a person could learn all knowledge and yet amount to nothing. He could even lay down his life in martyrdom and not achieve anything of value . . . if he hath not love! We will achieve the highest goal in life if we have "genuine love". God's Highest Goal for us:

IS
TO LOVE
TO CARE
TO SHARE

If we love one another, we will care about one another and we will share our love with others. God bless us all.

Shared by:

Vada Caldwell

I Corinthians Chapter 13

Be of Good Courage

My body is so very tired and in much pain
I need your strength to flow thru me
I am so completely drained.
I cling to your promise

Psalm 31:24

All ye that hope in the Lord
Be of good courage, and He shall
strengthen your heart.
I promise dear Lord of mine
To quickly do my part.
I come to you, please make me thine.

Written by:
Vada Caldwell

Heart and Soul

We traveled up, up the mountain peak
Christ the Savior to seek.

Just as I am without one plea
Oh God I humbly pray to Thee
Forgive me dear God as I stand
Looking up and reaching for your healing hand.

I want with all my heart and soul
To follow Jesus Christ your beloved Son
And have Him make me whole.

God touched me and this I believe
He changed my life and His salvation I received.
Thank you dear Lord for your saving touch.

Written by:

Vada Caldwell

2016

Sentence Prayers

Sweet Holy Spirit fill us and thrill us with your light
you are the light of our world.

A heart of sin corrupted
May tell you that you are just
But Christ alone can save you.
In him put your trust.

You've heard people say
I can see God in the sky, land and sea
But my heart cries as I pray
Let others see Him in me.

Oh dear Lord
Each morning when first I awake
I embrace the hope of every new dawning.

It's always darkest before the dawn
Morning is all night coming -
But it does appear!

Christ will never let us down.
Christ will never let us go.
Christ gives abundant life
Christ is above all.
Christ is the Alpha (beginning) and Omega (ending).
Thank you God for all your blessings so freely given!

Shared by:

Vada Caldwell

2016

Mary Catherine Caldwell
Brooks Farr

Born 7/8/1951 . . .

To Heaven 11/19/2012

About My Baby Girl

My youngest child, Mary Catherine was born on Sunday July 8, 1951, my love, my sweetness. An Irish saying states "The bairn (child) that is born on the Sabbath (Sunday) is bonny and blithe, and good and gay. That describes my daughter completely from the day of her birth. Cathy was always loving and kind with a heart so pure, gentle and caring. She always brought great joy into my life.

At the age of 18 she married Jerry Brooks. Two beautiful girls were born, Amy Christine and Rebecca Leigh. Her life was centered around her two precious children and their happiness. Their needs and desires came first. She joined the church, the girls accepted Christ and were baptized. The three of them attended Church. Cathy had a beautiful voice and sang in the choir, often lending her voice in solo presentations. After 18 years, Jerry and Cathy were divorced. She attended Memphis State and earned her degree in education. She became a teacher of excellence in the Shelby County school system. My daughter was dedicated to her students and quickly won their respect and love. Everyone loved her. She was my pride and joy for all she had worked for and accomplished.

Even though it took hours of diligence in her work, she made sure the needs and happiness of her girls still came first. They lived with me and her Dad for a period of time as she struggled to raise them to be good and live responsible lives. In my heart and sight Cathy was always my baby and brought me and her Daddy great joy.

She married again to Raymond Farr on June 15, 1991. Due to poor health and financial problems another struggle began. I prayed and cried asking God to care for her. By this time the girls were grown and doing well on their own. Becky was married with three boys, Lucian, Julian and Matteo. They captured their grandmother's heart. She loved them so much she would have gladly given her life for them.

She loved her Father in Heaven, and in faith gave him her heart at a very early age and promised to serve Him. Our Heavenly Father called her home November 19, 2012. She was mine and now is His.

Vada Caldwell - 2016

Cathy Caldwell

Cathy Caldwell with
Uncle Vernon Henson

Becky, Cathy and
Amy Brooks

Amy, Cathy and
Becky Brooks

My Family

God has blessed me with a good wholesome life. I have experienced times of joy and times of sorrow. I lived a happy childhood with normal activities. I was blessed with a loving father and mother and two brothers and one sister. We had days of fun and laughter and even days of fighting. We were poor people but did not know it. We were wealthy in love and happiness.

I fell in love at age 15, married Thomas H. Caldwell, Jr. when I was 18. I gave birth to three children; two girls Cynthia Anne and Mary Catherine and a son Thomas H. Caldwell, III. They brought much happiness to our lives as well as worry as they grew older and experienced the normal teen age life. We traveled a lot as a family, had a good and happy life with many enjoyable vacations. When the children married and had children of their own making us grand-parents, we continued to spend times together. We often had family gatherings where everyone joined together for special days of love and caring. The family continued to grow. We were blessed again and again as more grandchildren came along.

Cindy and Ron had three children, Ronnie, Johnny and Pam.

Tommy and Nancy had three children, Sam, Lorrie Beth and Russell. Cancer took the life of our beloved Nancy during Lorrie Beth's pregnancy. Tommy later married Tammie Trojanavich. She came into our family sharing her life and love with all of us. She quickly became close to Sam, Lorrie Beth, Russell and me. We lost our precious Lorrie Beth to the horrible disease cancer. Tammie has won all our hearts and she has fallen in love with each one of us. Our family relationship with one another has grown into one of genuine love and friendship.

Cathy and Jerry had two girls, Amy and Becky.
We often had special times at our home with all of our family, for birthdays, Halloween, Thanksgiving, Christmas and Easter. The grandchildren all loved their Mamaw and their Papaw. We loved all of

them too, they were our life. Then great grandchildren were born and enriched our lives even more.

Ronnie Pritchard became the father of Stephen, Meghan and Christopher. He later married Sherrie who had three sons Michael, Brandon and Donald. Michael Sisco married Chelsey.

Johnny became the father of Savannah and Nathaniel, also of Jonathan and Haydyn. As a young boy he was special to me and his grandfather. He filled us with pride when he earned his Eagle Scout badge. He is a good and caring Dad to his children.

Pam married Billy Hoskins, he had two girls Hannah and Madison from a previous marriage. The two of them together became parents of Kaitlyn, B. J. and Taylor.

Granddaughter Sam gave birth to our great grandchild Wyatt Rich. She later married Len Sheppard and gave birth to a son Cobin. Len had two sons Brad and Logan.

Lorrie Beth married Al Leach. She gave birth to a son A.J. who was her special love and treasure. Cancer took her from us in 2014 leaving a void in our hearts and life but planting a flower in Heaven.

Russell grew up into a special young man. He is a loving and thoughtful father to his son Brody. He is presently a policeman (a member of the swat team.) Like his father, he lives an exemplary life.

Cathy's daughter Amy has always been a free spirit filled with love and laughter. We thought she would never marry because she enjoyed her independence. But…she met the love of her life and married Julio Zuniga. They own their home and restaurant and have a happy and successful life. Her mother would be so proud of her and happy for her. A heart attack ended Cathy's life and God took her home on November 19, 2012. Our hearts are lost without her.

Becky married Jason Severs and they are blessed with three precious boys, Lucian, Julian and Matteo. They own a restaurant and recently bought a new home. We respect and love them for their accomplishments. Becky and Amy's mother Cathy is looking down on them from Heaven with great joy and pride.

Then Great-Great Grandchildren were born:
Stephen and Alisa Pritchard became parents of Elizabeth
Meghan Pritchard gave birth to Maleah
Savannah Pritchard gave birth to Kaylee
Step Grandson Brandon Harris became the father of Ava Grace
Step Grandson Donnie Equires became the father of Konala

Times changed, lives became busier and busier. Fewer and fewer
family gatherings were held. We are separated by miles. Cindy and
Ron live with me in my home. Tommy and my beloved daughter-in-law
Tammie live next door, it is my joy to have them close by.
Al and A. J. live next door to Tommy and Tammie.
Sam and Len and their family live in Brighton, Tn.
Russell and his son Brody live in Arlington, Tn.
Ronnie and Sherrie and her boys and families live in Mississippi.
Stephen, Meghan and Christopher live in California.
Johnny lives in Memphis. Jonathan and Haydyn live in Memphis with
their mother. Savannah and Nathaniel live in Indiana.
Pam, Billy and children live in Millington.
Amy and Julio live in Memphis.
Becky and Jason with their children live in Memphis.

We all live busy lives but our love still abides with one another and our
Lord. Even though I do not see all of my family as often as I would like
they are never out of my heart or thoughts.

I remember each and every one of them in my prayers every single day
calling their name to God.

May God bless and keep us safe within His care today and every day is
my prayer.

From the heart of:

Mrs. Thomas H. Caldwell, Jr.

September 10, 2016

Dear God Heal Our Land

With all my heart and being I pray for our country. I pray for you and me and all our families. I pray for all people throughout the world. There has never been a time when prayer was needed more.

In the Bible II Chronicles 7:14 God speaks, He says:
If my people which are called by my name, shall
humble themselves, and pray, and seek my face and
turn from their wicked ways; then will I hear from
Heaven, and will forgive their sins and will heal their land.

If ever our land has needed the healing touch of our loving God, it is now. God always meets us at the point of our need. He gives us the joy of His presence every minute of every day. He invites us to come walk with him and serve him.

We must humble ourselves before God and pray at all times and in every situation. As we come to God in humility and prayer he has promised to heal our land. What is our land? Is it the world around us or could it be our families who have fallen away from God? God will use our humble prayers, he will answer and heal our land for He is always faithful to his promise.

If I fail to be humble and if I fail to pray, then I fail God. Blessed Lord help me to be humble before God and pray so I might be used as his instrument.

My prayer is that my life will develop more each day spiritually and never reach the point where I would stand still as a Christian. Never let me be satisfied with me. May I always strive onward and upward for Christ Jesus.

Help me to be an example to all who see me that Christians are not only happy and loving people thru Christ Jesus, but I believe a true Christian is truly a rare and beautiful creature to behold.

May we all be His people which are called by His Name!

Vada Henson Caldwell

Our Life of Special Memories

My husband Tommy had a massive stroke on October 24, 2001 which changed our life completely. After brain surgery, he spent many months in the hospital intensive care then to rehab hospital where he received little help. He was paralyzed, unable to walk but blessed with a clear mind.

I was told I would not be able to care for him at home. But I took him home after a miserable thirty days in a nursing home where he received very poor care.

On December 1, 2001 while sitting beside his hospital bed, we had one of our many conversations after his stroke. I had been reading while he slept. He awoke and said, Vada? I answered What darling? How did you learn so much in such a little time? Are you talking about me taking care of you and changing your diaper? He said "Yes". I told him, I had learned by watching others. He said a lot of it you learned on your own though.

I learned to love you a long time ago. Did you know you are the most important part of my life. He said, No, but I know you take pretty good care of me. His beautiful blue eyes searched mine and their memory is now burned into my heart.

I said, You are my precious one and I love you very much. He replied, I love you too Vada.

I thank God for my Tommy and Memories.

I miss him so very much, then I think of memories like this and my heart sings.

Vada Caldwell - 2016

Memories of
Vada Henson Caldwell

I remember a big, big house where Grandpa Charlie Yopp lived. I remember the biggest bookcase I ever saw standing in the hallway of this house and the excitement it held for me. It was like a treasure hunt to sit before the bookcase and look at the books. I loved books then, when I was a little child, and I still love and appreciate a good book. I remember in that same big house there was a room off the back porch that was filled with intrigue. It was a room with trunks, boxes and clothes hanging on hangers and lots of mysterious things. It was one of my favorite spots in my Grandpa's house.

I remember a bed so soft that I would just sink down, down, down into the feather bed and sleep so good and feel so safe and warm when I spent the night at my Grandpa's house.

I remember the pond down behind the barn. It would freeze over in the winter time and those who were not afraid would try to skate across the frozen ice.

I remember hog killing time, and I remember the 'smokehouse' where the hams hung and looked so strange. And I remember a huge, gigantic mulberry tree in the backyard with the biggest, juiciest most luscious berries.

I remember my Aunt LaVelle's 'Hope Chest', the most beautiful piece of furniture I had ever seen. It had a tray that would lift up and out. Aunt LaVelle Yopp would let me touch the soft, silk things she had inside and show me her treasures. I am sure it was at this time the dream was born in my heart of owning a cedar chest one day of my very own.

174

Oh, and I remember one Christmas after my Aunt LaVelle had moved to Nashville to work, we received a package from her. It was a box filled with pencils. They each had nice sharp points and a good eraser. These were pencils used at her workplace until they became too short to be held comfortably and then were discarded. My aunt's employer let her save them for us. This was one of the most exciting and unusual gifts we ever had and gave each of us hours of joy.

And then there was the orchard. In my eyes it just had to be the biggest orchard ever. There were trees of every kind, apple, peach, pears, and plums. We spent many times of fun and laughter as we walked through the orchard and picked the fruit from the trees.

Late one afternoon, my Uncle Wilford came riding up on his horse with a sack filled with apples and pears. He calmly announced, "Sis, I have brought you some apples and pears and I have come to live with you."

I spent the night with my Uncle Nathan and Aunt Mary Joe Yopp not long after they were married. They lived in the old home place, a long rambling house and made me feel so loved and were so much fun to be with.

I accidentally saw my Aunt Lola and her boy friend Sam Barr kissing each other goodnight, and she said, "Don't tell Sis, but it is all right because we are going to get married."

I remember a childhood in the country community of Roger Springs, Tennessee. I remember my Daddy and my Mother and the love they had for their children and what a happy family we were.

I remember going to singing conventions every year with Mama and Daddy. The conventions were held in small towns nearby and people gathered from miles to sing. I thought my Mother and Daddy could sing better than anyone else. My Daddy had a sweet, beautiful tenor voice which rang out above all others. Mother's voice was clear as a bell and I could find her in a crowd by listening for her beautiful alto voice.

My Mother was and still is a gentle woman with a quiet beauty of her own and a steadfast faith in her God. My Daddy was a big, strong man, yet gentle and kind. He was a great hunter and lover of dogs and the outdoor life. In my eyes, he could do no wrong for in my mind, he was the king of all men.

My life in the country was simple and what seemed to be uneventful. But now as I look back and can remember many things that happened over the years, I realize it was filled with events of excitement, a full life close to nature and God.

I remember finding a litter of puppies being born and the wonder of it all. I remember a chicken snake in the hen house and how funny it looked after it swallowed the round door knobs used for a setting egg. A pet coon named Sambo – and my Daddy's tears when he told me the dogs had killed my Sambo. I remember the times of fun and excitement when I went hunting with my Daddy.

Yes, I remember with great joy all of these times. Then I remember with sorrow when I think of those whom I have loved who have gone from this world. Yet I can remember with Praise that I know where they are.

A little talk my Daddy and I had at the hospital one day just before he died has always stayed with me. Very few days have gone by in my life that I have not thought of his words. "If you love someone, tell them now --- if you are proud of someone, tell them now. I am so proud of you and the young lady you have turned out to be. In all you ever do, always be a lady and I will never have any reason not to be proud of you."

Then my memories would not be complete if I did not say, that I remember meeting a young man with clear blue eyes, who became my husband. His name is Tommy Caldwell and God gave us three beautiful children and six precious grandchildren. With #7 on the way!

If you love someone, tell them now!

I love you and pray God's blessings upon each of you forevermore.

Lovingly,

Vada

Written in 1981

?

176

School Bus - Route
Country to Middleton
High School

'The Old School Bus'

Every day my Daddy, L. D. Henson drove the school bus to Middleton High School. We traveled over dirt roads, dusty and hot in the summer time. And muddy, slippery soapstone roads in the cold, cold winter.

The trip was long and tiring. Often Daddy would have to stop the bus and separate some of the kids from fighting. More times than I care to remember, I was one of the kids fighting.

When I was bad, Daddy would stop the bus and make me move to the front and sit beside him the rest of the way home or to school whichever it happened to be. The only problem with that type of punishment was that I really liked to sit by my Daddy.

Sometimes, I was bad on purpose just so I could sit with my Daddy.

Vada Henson Caldwell

Terror in the Night as Remembered

One afternoon my brother Roy, my sister Maggie Ruth and I walked up the road about a mile to visit our Aunt Annie Pearl and Uncle Charlie Yopp. They always treated us special and we had a great time visiting. This day we were enjoying ourselves so much we stayed so long it was beginning to turn dark when we left for home.

We were skipping along, laughing and singing on our way. We always thought making noise would keep us from getting scared in the dark. As it grew darker, the moon began shining and creating shadows on the road.

In the moonlight, the ground was suddenly covered by two grotesque shadows made even more frightening by a flapping sound like the wings of a giant condor and the howl of an angry animal.

The three of us screamed in terror. Roy grabbed one of my arms and Maggie Ruth the other, and with all the strength they had to call upon ran from the road over the fields, through the bushes, briar patches and over barbed wire fences pulling me between them until we reached the safety of home and the protecting arms of Mama and Daddy.

Our clothes were torn, our legs and arms covered with scratches and cuts. Each of us gasped for breath as we tried to tell our story. Washed and loved and comforted, we were put to bed for the night.

The next day Mr. Dixon and his son came to tell Daddy they were the ones who scared us and to apologize.

They said they saw our shadows on the road just as we saw theirs and playfully slapped the sides of their legs and growled. They called after us as we ran but their voices were drowned out by our screams. What they meant for fun turned out to be a time of fear for me, my brother and sister. They were so sorry, so we forgave them.

Written by: Vada Henson Caldwell

Memories

One of my first memories of school in Middleton, Tenn. As best I can remember I was in the second grade and our teacher had a rule concerning her leaving the room for some reason. She always appointed one of the students to take charge in her absence and report to her if anyone left their chair while she was gone.

One day she left a girl named Ann Keith in charge. I cannot remember if I talked or moved from my chair. I do remember Ann drew a circle on the blackboard with chalk. She pushed my nose against it and ordered me to stand there till the teacher returned. I remember the humiliation I felt as all the other children laughed at me.

Strange as it seems, I don't remember the teacher's reaction when she returned, nor do I remember her name or the name of any of the other classmates. To this day I do not know why I was chosen for this punishment. Perhaps because I was smaller and Ann had been given a power too big for her to understand. I do remember that from that day forward I could not stand to be around her.

We lived in the rural area several miles from the highway which we traveled to get to the school. We rode in a wagon with benches on each side. The cover was made of a coarse brown tarpaulin material and the cold air and wind still penetrated through and crept in through the corners and doorway making it very cold. The dirt roads were mostly red clay. When it rained the clay became very slippery. The poor horses labored along the clay roads and the sound of their hoofs struggling to walk sounded similar to that of a suction cup being pulled loose. As the winter months grew colder, the road became harder and harder for the horses and wagon to travel. As the horses staggered under their burden, the wagon wheels crunched the cold hard ground beneath. With each step it was a struggle for the horses to free their imprisoned feet from the clinging clay, it was an experience for us and the horses.

Vada

Life in the Country

We lived in a sparsely populated rural area, there were only a few houses and they were miles apart. The nearest town to our house was Roger Springs, Tennessee. It consisted of two small grocery stores, a train stop, the Post Office and a gasoline tank.

On a hillside three miles away stood a little one room Church of Christ with a cemetery across the dirt road. Our family attended the church. Our transportation was a mule drawn wagon. On Sunday morning Daddy would hook up the team and we would take off for the church. My Daddy was the song leader and had a golden voice that spread the most beautiful music throughout the church and country side. Everyone said I was Daddy's pet, maybe I was and then maybe I wasn't. He loved my sister Maggie Ruth very much, a pretty girl with golden curls and a voice like an angel. She sang for us, sang for company and at church. Daddy bragged on her to everyone. With a laugh, he often said this is my daughter, I can make her do anything she wants to. He also loved me very much and did spoil me. I thought he was the most wonderful person that ever lived.

My brother Roy was born with a God given talent for music and art. He could hear a song and then play it without missing a beat. We did not have the money to buy him a piano, so whenever we visited anyone who had one, he would sit down and start playing.

My Daddy made part of our living in trading cattle, dogs, you name it. One day he came home with a big smile and called for all of us to see what he brought home. It was so exciting, he had traded a broken mirror for an old pump organ. Roy, sat down, pumped that organ and made the most beautiful music. Every evening we would all gather around that organ and while Roy played we would sing. It was a time of family sharing which lasted a long time.

One day Roy was playing the old pump organ and it just stopped. He kicked it and it fell apart, he started crying. Daddy said don't worry about it son. It will probably make good kindling. My brother Vernon took it outside, picked up the axe and chopped it into pieces, that was the last of our instrumental music. We just laughed and kept on singing…

When the Roll Is Called Up Yonder.

Ten miles away was the bigger town of Middleton. The High School was located there and had classes from First grade through Twelfth. There was also one grocery store, a ten cent store, pool hall, beauty and barber shop. A small restaurant, hardware store and train station. Two churches, one Church of Christ and one Methodist.

There was one brick house on a hill across the road from the Post Office. A few plain wooden houses scattered around the area. It seemed to me as a child it was lots of beautiful homes, both wood and brick. There were only about ten houses in the township. A Baptist church was on the side of a road about half way between the two towns.

Our family lived in a plain board house my Daddy had built. It was about ten miles from Roger Springs. We sometimes walked along the railroad tracks to go to town. Our house was nothing fancy but was made into a beautiful home by the love abiding there. Honoring one another and worshipping God. My Daddy had a beautiful voice and led the singing in the Church of Christ every Sunday.

Our material possessions were few but our lives were filled
with wonder and adventure. We were ordinary people living
extra-ordinary lives.

Written by: Vada Henson Caldwell

Vada, Vernon, Roy and Maggie Ruth Henson

Our Mama, Wilma Henson, Vada, Maggie Ruth and house my Daddy built for us in Roger Springs, TN

Little Grandmother Henson, My Mother Wilma Yopp Henson and house my Daddy built for Grandma in Roger Springs, TN

My Daddy L.D. Henson, Speaker &
Jack ready to go hunting

Vada Henson and Speaker going
hunting with my Daddy, 9 years old

Moving to the City

When I was twelve years old, my sister and brother graduated from high school in Middleton. Tennessee. My Mother and Daddy decided it was time to move to Memphis to better ourselves. My oldest brother Vernon had quit school and moved away. Mama, Daddy, Roy and Maggie Ruth moved to Memphis …without me…! It broke my heart. I was sent to spend the summer with my Aunt Maggie and Uncle Tom until the family could get settled and have a place for me. They all moved into a boarding house to live while looking for work. Daddy went to work for Ford Motor Company as a Security Guard, my Mother worked for Goldsmiths Department Store.

One day my sister Maggie Ruth left early to go downtown to look for a job, they hired her on the spot. She had been gone all morning and early afternoon returned to the boarding house almost in tears. She said, "I got a job, worked all morning, went to lunch and now I can't find it". The owner of the boarding house helped her find it.

My folks rented the "biggest house" I had ever seen, it was located at 2007 Oliver and we moved in just before my 13th birthday. I was one happy young girl when we traveled to Memphis with our belongings and moved into the house.

One of the first things my Daddy did was go buy a piano for my brother Roy. Mama decided she would give music lessons to Roy. She had heard about a German Music Teacher who gave lessons in his home at a nominal fee. She made arrangements to take Roy to see him. The teacher said to Roy, sit down and play something for me. He began to play, first "Ah Sweet Mystery of Life, Schubert's Symphony and Indian Love Call". The teacher looked at Mama and said, I could take your money and give your son lessons, but I would only be doing you a disservice. Your son already has a talent the good Lord has given him and I would only be ruining that God given ability and talent. Mama thanked him and she and Roy came home.

School started in June and I started the 9th grade at Fairview Junior High. Did not know anyone and felt completely out of place. I was a country girl in a big city school. Met a girl named Hazel Duke and we became friends. She lived across the street from Lona Lovett and we became friends as well.

On March 3, 1944 Hazel was spending the night with me, her boyfriend Virgil called and wanted to come over. I asked my Mother if it would be all right. She said since she was home it would be ok, then he said he had a friend who would like to come with him and meet me. Mama said all right but we could not go anywhere else. We were having a good time and my sister Maggie Ruth and brother Roy came home early. We enjoyed visiting and talking with one another, then I asked Roy to play the piano. He began to play and we all started singing and we had a great time. I met Tommy Caldwell that night and hoped I would see him again. My wish came true, he called the next day and we became girlfriend and boyfriend.

We moved to 816 Loeb Street near the Kennedy Veterans Hospital. The name of the street where the hospital was located at that time was Shotwell. They changed the name to Getwell which seemed more appropriate.

This was a new sub-division, so we were all strangers. It did not take long for all of us to become acquainted and good neighbors. We were blessed with a closeness which was unusual for the city, but our little street was more like the country.

I started the 10th grade at Tech High, I rode a city bus to crosstown then transferred to a street car. I knew very few people at Tech, was shy and did not make friends easily. Of course Hazel and Lona were still my friends, but went to a different school after I moved.

My favorite subjects were typing and shorthand. I excelled at typing and won ribbons. While I was in first year typing my teacher had me take a test with his second year class. To my delight I won the test and received a blue ribbon.

Another exciting part of my high school years happened in my senior year. My shorthand teacher gave each of us the assignment of answering an ad for a job. I answered an ad of Memphis Steam Laundry. My teacher mailed the letter and to my surprise I received a call asking me to come to work the next week. I accepted the job making a salary of $12.00 per week.

We had a happy life during these times. Though we had both sad and happy times, but that is the way our Lord has planned life to be.

We were a loving family with consideration and kindness for one another. Our life was made even more special with our mutual love for music. Almost every day, at twilight my brother Roy would begin playing the piano and the rest of us would gather around and sing at the top of our voices. The music could be heard all through the neighborhood. Doors would open, chairs would assemble on porches and the lawn as our neighbors joined together to hear the Henson family making music ring.

My grandfather Henson got pneumonia and died on my Daddy's 18th birthday. A very sad time for all the family. My grandmother was left with six children, so my Daddy worked and helped his mother care for the other children. His brothers and sisters lovingly called him "D".

My grandmother named my Daddy L. D. Henson and said if she were to give him a name it would be Lorenzo Dow after the famous preacher.

My "Little Mamaw" as I called her had much influence upon my life. She taught me how to laugh, cry, love and live. She was a really good person.

In 1945 and 1946, my Daddy L. D. Henson struggled with the dreaded disease of cancer. On October 2, 1946 God called him home, saying I have prepared a place for you, there will be no more pain, come unto me my good and faithful servant.

I was 18 years old and married when Daddy died. He was laid to rest in the cemetery across the dirt road from the Church of Christ where during his life he served God for many years.

The church did not have indoor plumbing, there was an outhouse in the woods behind the church. We had to walk thru the woods to get there. Others were waiting so my grandmother said let's walk behind the outhouse, no one will be looking. She said you know what they always say…speak no evil, hear no evil and see no evil. Then with a smile and a little laugh in her voice, she said with her hands on her face and her fingers spread apart, "Lots of times, I have been tempted to peek".

This from my precious grandmother whose heart was
breaking because her son was gone.

My beloved Daddy was gone and I wept as my heart ached.

As I write these words, my heart is filled with pride, joy, sorrow
and praise. I praise my God for the memories and thank Him for
His constant and everlasting love and presence.

Written by:

Vada Henson Caldwell

Started years ago and finished

October 28, 2016

Love Grows

Love is wonderful and strange
It's power can transform and re-arrange
The lives of those to whom it is expressed.
In word or deed – in times of happiness or deep distress.

Love plants into every heart the seed
of hope and everlasting joy.
Love can heal a persons need.

Love, like faith, can grow
from a very tiny seed
Through nurture and feeding upon
God's Word!

Written by:

Vada Caldwell

October 2016

God Gives Life

God gave me life
He promised to be with me all my days.
Whether they be filled with peace or strife.
He gave me life filled with sunshine rays.

God gave me a family
Whose love has grown from generation to generation.
A New Dawn greets me each day.
In this gloriously beautiful nation.

The morning is new.
The sky is blue.
The grass is green.
God is still the King.

Death has taken many from this earth
They now dwell in Heaven
A reward for their new birth.

By: Vada Caldwell - October, 2016

To Jesus I Talked

I cannot say this day,
I walked where Jesus walked
But Oh Dear God. I can say
Today with Jesus I talked.

I listened to those with blessings and
burdens to share.
My cares were lifted away
As I gave them all to Him in prayer
And asked Him to strengthen my life
from day to day.

In my heart the living Christ is real
And oh what a Heavenly thrill
I felt the Hand of God touch me
I rose from a little hill
To the limb of the tallest tree.

I knew that God was listening to my prayer
For I felt His Presence there!

Written by: Vada Henson Caldwell

Jesus Christ and Us

Emerson said, "Of what use is eternity if a man doesn't know how to use a half hour?"

All the great people of history and today find time to draw apart to enjoy quiet and solitude. We will work for the Master, we will even sing, preach and teach. Sometimes though we need to be still so we can feel the power of God through peace and quiet with Christ.

Moses drew apart.
Paul of Tarsus was alone on a lonely stretch of the road at the time of his conversion. Jesus Christ drew apart to pray.

Let us – "Be Still and Know That I Am God." (Psalm 46) We will grow in Spirit and in Knowledge as we seek our Lord.

Vada Caldwell

I begin my day in a time of quiet and prayer. I invite you to try it and find peace.

Heaven's Flowers

Watch the flowers of Heaven grow
As others toil below
Then to replenish the flowers on earth
God performed a miracle of birth.

This is God's plan
The marvelous goal of our God
He takes one of His above
And brings another for us to cherish and love.
While still upon His earth we trod.

Written by:

Vada Caldwell

2016

San Antonio, Texas...April, 1951...Cynthia Anne Caldwell, Wilma Yopp Henson, Vada Henson Caldwell and Thomas Herbert Caldwell, III...Happy Days... Cathy on the way

My Mama, Annie Wilma Yopp, as a School Teacher 16 years of age

My Mother Annie Wilma Yopp Henson

Memories of Life

Growing up in the country gave me a firm foundation for my life. I had two older brothers and a sister. Our Mother and Father were simple farm people with a deep love for their family, home and God.

Our meals were referred to as breakfast, dinner and supper. Although it was often simple fare, we gathered around the kitchen table, always eating together. Sharing in joy and laughter.

My Mother now lives with me. Her meals are still breakfast, dinner and supper. She has scrambled eggs for breakfast, meat and vegetables for dinner and Special K with a banana for supper. Every morning before I leave for work, I prepare her dinner trying to have a variety of meat and vegetables.

Each evening when I come home from work I say, hello Mama how was your day? Almost always her reply is Oh, just about the same as usual. After our greeting and talking a little, I go to the kitchen to prepare supper. She looks forward to her supper and enjoys it more than any meal.

With the first sound of activity in the kitchen, I can count on hearing my Mother's voice calling, "Vada". I go to her and say, "Yes Mama did you call me?" She says, "I wanted to know how long will it be before I can have my Special K? Soon Mother, soon. As soon as it is prepared, I go get her and bring her into the kitchen. I watch my Mother (who is now my child) as she lifts her spoon with trembling hands and I turn my back so she will not see my tears. The tears always flow as I remember the gentle, loving hands that have cared for me all my life.

Then I smile within as I remember her daily question - Now how long will it be till I can have my Special K?

In Memory of My Beloved Mama, Annie Wilma Yopp Henson

By: Vada Henson Caldwell

Thomas Herbert Caldwell, Jr.

1945

Cynthia Anne Caldwell
1967 Graduation
Hillcrest High School
Memphis, TN

Thomas Herbert
Caldwell, III
1968 Graduation
Hillcrest High School
Memphis, TN

Mary Catherine Caldwell
1969 Graduation
Hillcrest High School
Memphis, TN

Labor of Love

The creation of this book has been a true labor of love. I have attempted to share my life with you and to honor my parents for the life they lived and their love and struggles experienced in raising we four children. They taught us to worship and obey God in our daily lives. By example they taught us to be decent, hardworking, honest and caring human beings.

I thank my family for their joint labor of love with me.

My beloved husband, Thomas H. Caldwell, Jr.
And my three children:

Cynthia Anne Caldwell Pritchard
Thomas Herbert Caldwell, III
Mary Catherine Caldwell Brooks Farr

I thank God for the times of joy and sorrow we shared with one another over the years.

Vada H. Caldwell

November 3, 2016

My Life at Kellogg Company

By

Vada Caldwell

1959 to 1990

The Journey

In March of 1959 I drove to Kellogg Company in Memphis, Tennessee to apply for work. I was given an application to complete. When finished, the Personnel Manager interviewed me then asked if I could begin work the next day. With great joy I answered yes. On March 22, 1959 I began my journey with Kellogg Company which lasted thirty years.

I began as a clerk in the General Office. There were three shifts of employees in the plant: 7am to 3pm, 3pm to 11pm, 11pm to 7am. My duties were recording manually the number of cases of cereal produced by each shift, then combining all shifts. A few months later I was given the job of Payroll clerk. It was a good company to work for and I enjoyed the work.

I changed jobs over the years, accounts payable, bookkeeper, relief clerk which entailed purchasing, personnel, PBX operator and other clerical positions. I retired April 30, 1990 as Accounts Payable Bookkeeper.

Through the days, weeks, months and years I was blessed with numbers of friends. Many continue to be my friends after all these years reflecting the words of our founder W. K. Kellogg:

KELLOGG'S IS PEOPLE!

I am thankful for my life with Kellogg Company and the life and friends I enjoy now. I Praise my God from whom all blessings flow.

Vada Henson Caldwell

Artie Byrd,
Executive VP-
Operations
Kellogg USA

Vada Caldwell,
Accts Payable
Bookkeeper

Becky Clark,
Administrative
Assistant

Ken Lindsey, General
Office Manager

Bill Porter, General
Plant Manager

March 9, 1985

Written by Vada Caldwell

Kellogg Corporate Annual Review

Holiday Inn Conference Center

Olive Branch, Mississippi

A Poem of Greetings

Once again at our Annual Meeting
We extend to each of you a special greeting!

The things we've seen
The words we've heard
Have our memories stirred
of the pledge last year by our team.

We were committed to growth in 84!
Day by day, all year through
To our pledge we proved to be true
We strived, we worked, we grew more and more.

When we look back upon our Kellogg history.
We find a giant of the cereal industry.
John Harvey Kellogg, doctor, author and director
of the Battle Creek 'San'
Hired his brother Will Keith to work by his side
Dr. John in his book "Man The Masterpiece" devoted chapters
to the cure and treatment of the maladies of man
of which he strongly professed his belief in the prevention to be
Proper diet, consistent exercise, no strong drink and the
practice of Christianity.

The first cereal flake was formed
quite by accident when the brothers two
developed a food of grain for health
for the patients at the Sanitarium.

Their discoveries progressed from cereal foods
to bread substitutes made from wheat.
All the patients said, "It sure tastes good"
and when released wrote for more of this special food to eat.

For twenty-five years, Dr. John, the older one
held Will Keith beneath his thumb.
All Will's urging to go into business was to no avail.
At the age of 50, Will Keith was determined to show brother John
So he left the employ of his brother and The San
For he knew he could not fail
and said within his heart, "I know I can".

His cereal business quickly grew from 35 cases per day to 2900.
He improved upon the processes used before.
The people began to buy more and more,
Above all else, his courage shone.
When he advertised…Please stop eating toasted Corn Flakes
for 30 days, so your friends and neighbors all around
can have a chance to buy and taste what you have found.

So our founder, Will Keith Kellogg
Stepped from beneath the shadow of brother John.
And in developing foods of grain for better health
Built an empire of untold wealth!

With determination he set out to show John it could be done
He proved himself by going the distance
In both production and advertising of excellence
Reached out to deliver the difference.

Knowing the steps of such a man
Could we do less than say, "Yes we can"
And work throughout the year of 1985
To honor our founder, by delivering the difference.

This Is Your Life
William A. Porter

You've heard it said, I know a man is known by his good measure
So tonight it gives me great pleasure
To share with you this man's life.
Bill Porter come forward with your wife,
For now we present – "THIS IS YOUR LIFE".

It was Spokane, Washington where he first appeared on this earth
October 9, 1922 was the date of his birth.
Margaret and Frank were proud parents of child number four
For a brother and twin sisters had been born before.
Everybody said a baby that can cry that loud, is sure to make us proud.

Gonzages High School was his Alma Mater
And at football there was none greater
As a senior he was All City Football Captain of the Year,
A title of pride and great cheer.
An atheletic scholarship at the time of his graduation
Made Eastern Washington College his next step in education.

It was in Omaha, Nebraska where he first began
As a member of the Kellogg clan.
Twenty-four years was his age,
When employed by Kellogg's at their minimum wage.
In 1947 he was sweeping the floor
But soon they found him to be capable of much more.
So Quality Control Foreman was the promotion
Which really started his climb into motion.

This young man learned more and more each day
And, of course, deserved an increase in pay
And those who counted, so noted
Thus in 1950 to Food Foreman he was promoted.

Another step was made toward his place in the sun
When he became Quality Control Supervisor in 1951.
Still another reason this year stands out in his life
Is the fact he met the girl he wanted for his wife.
He begged, "Won't you join me in Wedded Bliss?"
Her answer of "Yes" was sealed with a kiss.

As though it was the hand of fate
Just three years after the day they met
September 18, 1954 for the Wedding Day was set
"Till death do us part" was the vow of each mate.

Along came the children to add to their joy,
The first born, a girl named Lynn
Then along came Kemper, a little boy
With a team like this they were sure to win.

A little over ten years ago, it was plain to see
There would be a Kellogg Plant in Memphis, Tennessee.
So this is a time to remember and celebrate
For as destiny would have it in the year 1958
The need for Quality Control Supervisor in Memphis arose,
Bill Porter, of course, was the one they chose.
So in October of this famous year,
Our own Bill Porter was sent to us here.

His accomplishments continued to show through,
So he was made Production Supervisor in January 1962.
He worked day and night to learn all the tricks,
And went forward to Production Manager in March of 1966.

And now because the job in San Leandro
Calls for nothing less than a pro,
Bill is leaving our town
To serve as Plant Manager, a job of renown.

This poem has been filled with an amount of mirth,
So to add to it a quality of worth,
Bill, we all want you to know as we bid you adieu
The people in Memphis will never forget you.

Written by Mrs. Tommy Caldwell, Jr. (Vada)

During first two weeks of February, 1969.

To be presented at a "Going Away Dinner Party on February 15, 1969

This Is Your Life
Ken Lindsey

March 18, 1988

IN HOMER, MICHIGAN ON JUNE 30, 1931
AN ONLY CHILD WAS BORN TO BLAYNE AND BERTHA LINDSEY.
WITH JOY THEY LOOKED UPON THEIR LITTLE SON.
HIS NAME WAS KENNETH RONALD LINDSEY.
THEY BEAMED WITH PRIDE AS THEY WATCHED HIM GROW.
HIS FIRST STEPS WERE TINY AND SLOW.

TOO SOON, HE WAS OLD ENOUGH TO GO TO SCHOOL.
AN HONOR STUDENT THROUGHOUT THE YEARS,
HE ALWAYS FOLLOWED THE "GOLDEN RULE".
THEIR PRIDE AND LOVE SHONE THROUGH JOYFUL TEARS
AS THEY WATCHED HIM GRADUATE FROM HOMER HIGH IN 1949.

HE SERVED HIS COUNTRY IN THE UNITED STATES AIR FORCE.
RETURNED HOME TO MAP HIS LIFE'S FUTURE COURSE.
COLLEGE IN FORT WAYNE, INDIANA WAS THE PLACE
HE WOULD EQUIP HIMSELF FOR THE RACE.

IT WAS THERE HE MET THE LOVE OF HIS LIFE
AND BRAVELY ASKED HER TO BE HIS WIFE.
ON AUGUST 8, 1956, HAPPILY THEY WERE WED.
PROMISED TO BE FAITHFUL IN THE YEARS AHEAD.

IN 1962 THE BIRTH OF STEVE, THEIR FIRST BABY BOY
ADDED GREATLY TO THEIR ABOUNDING JOY.
THE BIRTH OF GREG IN 1964
MADE THEM COUNT THEIR BLESSINGS MORE AND MORE.

IT WAS BATTLE CREEK, MI WHERE HIS KELLOGG CAREER BEGAN.
ACCTS PAYABLE CLERK WAS THE FIRST POSITION FOR THIS YOUNG MAN.
PAYABLES CLERK, ACCOUNTANT, COST ACCOUNTANT.
PROMOTIONS CAME HIS WAY ONE BY ONE
AS HE WORKED TO MAKE HIS WAY IN THE SUN.

HE GREW IN KNOWLEDGE AS HE WORKED EACH DAY
AND BELIEVED IN A GOOD DAY'S WORK FOR A GOOD DAY'S PAY.

HIS WORK AND HIS ZEAL CONTINUED TO SHINE
AND HE MOVED FORWARD A STEP AT A TIME.
COST SUPERVISOR IN 1965 AT OMAHA, NE WAS HIS NEXT STEP.
MARVIN SMITH TRAINED HIM WELL AND IN DEPTH.

ON JUNE 2, 1969 HE CAME TO MEMPHIS, TENNESSEE.
PLANT CONTROLLER & GENERAL OFFICE MGR WAS THE POSITION.
THEN BEGAN THE GREAT 'TRANSITION' FROM "Yankee"
TO "Southern" – SUCCESSFULLY COMPLETED FOR ALL TO SEE.

KEN WALKED INTO THE MEM PLANT WITH ONE THING ON HIS MIND –
I'LL BE GOOD AT MY JOB AND SEE THAT OTHERS TOW THE LINE.

EVERY MORNING, OUR BREAK TIME WAS AT EIGHT.
HE COULD NOT BELIEVE IT AS WE WALKED DOWN THE HALL.
HE SAID, IT WOULD BE BETTER IF YOUR BREAKS YOU WOULD ROTATE.
BELIEVE ME, CHANGING HIM TOOK US QUITE A WHILE,
BUT NOW, KEN IS THE FIRST TO SAY WITH A SMILE
"LET'S TAKE A BREAK YA'LL".

EVEN THOUGH THE FURROWED BROW AND A TUG AT HIS COLLAR
WAS OUR CLUE HE WAS ABOUT TO HOLLER
IT'S TIME FOR THE WORK TO BEGIN,
KEN LINDSEY WAS A GOOD BOSS, BOTH FIRM AND FAIR
A MAN WITH A TENDER HEART, AND A COMPASSIONATE FRIEND.
HE WAS ALWAYS THERE TO CARE AND SHARE.

KEN, OUR WISH FOR YOU IS TIME TO TRAVEL, FISH, PLAY GOLF AND REST,
CAUSE WE THINK YOU DESERVE THE VERY BEST!
AS YOU MOVE FORWARD IN YOUR LIFE WITH CORINNE
MAY THE DAYS AND YEARS AHEAD BE KIND.
DON'T FORGET THOSE YOU LEAVE BEHIND.
FOR YOU WILL ALWAYS BE OUR FRIEND.

REGARDLESS OF WHAT ELSE YOU HEAR TONIGHT,
AS WE TELL YOU GOODBYE, SO LONG, FAREWELL AND ADIEU
WE HOPE THIS PARTY WILL GIVE YOU MEMORIES OF DELIGHT.
WE DO LOVE YOU, AND WE ARE GOING TO MISS YOU!

Written in Love,

By: Vada Caldwell

Tribute to My Kellogg Family

written by Vada Caldwell - 1993

To our life, memories have so much to give
And we will remember every day that we live
Our trip to Battle Creek in 1993
To reminisce with our boys from Tennessee;
Don Thomason, Artie Byrd, Bob Martin –
our friends forever
Should they become president or whatever!

Thanks to Senior Vice President Artie Byrd
The "Red Carpet" treatment we received
A welcome of such magnitude unbelieved.

A "special" two days and two nights
Eating, shopping, and seeing the sights
Every moment was perfectly swell
Each event and activity planned so very well.
What else can we possibly say
Except our thanks to Artie's secretary, Marsha Pompey!

There are many people in our land
Who could never, never understand
The treasures of friendship we have found
Or our closeness so profound.

Joy, smiles, and the sounds of laughter
Experienced as we travel will linger in our hearts long after!
Together we worked for many years
In joy and good health, sickness and sorrow
Sharing our hopes and our fears
Looking forward to each tomorrow
And now as our golden years unfold,
We share a friendship of wealth untold.

Thank you one and all for being my friend
I'll stand by you through thick and thin
This is very true,

For I love each one of you.

Kellogg Salaried Annual Meeting

January, 1977

Reach out in 77 is Kellogg's plan
And for many years we have heard it said
Kellogg's is People.

So, as people all over our land,
We reach out for Kellogg's.
It will be sure we will keep reaching out
To God and our fellowman!

Written by: Vada Caldwell

Annual Corporate Overview Meeting for all Kellogg Salaried Personnell

January 21, 1978

Welcome to our friends from Battle Creek
We sure are glad to have you here
We always look forward to this event of the year.

We in Memphis, pledge to go the distance and
excellence to pursue.
We also wish to pursue happiness for those of us
at home as well as all of you.

We are glad to be a part of the winning team
Who uphold the American dream
That happiness is living, loving and giving of ourselves
And excellence is Kellogg products on all our
kitchen shelves!

Written by: Vada Caldwell

Kellogg of Memphis

In World Wide Performance, Memphis is Number One
This accomplishment in the year of 1978 -
As 'Tony' would say was really grrreat!
Our people worked hard all thru the year of 1979
Now even greater — we keep the cup for a second time.

Twenty years ago Kellogg Company awarded the first
President's cup.
It has traveled to the Kellogg plants throughout the land.
Only Omaha has held the cup for a three year span.

The people of Memphis began to look up
And said — one day — we'll win that cup.
With pride together they decided to stand
As they answered the challenge with --- Yes We Can.
Worked with determination and began to Reach Out.
Teamwork just had to be what it was all about.

Good leadership and teams working hand in hand
Helped the Memphis plant reach their goal.
Such an accomplishment makes all of us feel grand,
For it takes every single one to make up the
Kellogg Plant as a whole.

Our goal for 1980 . . . just between you and me,
The President's Cup in Memphis . . . not just two years, but three.
If Omaha can do it, so can we.
For you see, in Memphis, WE ARE FAMILY!

Written By: Vada Caldwell

January 18, 1980

214

Annual Meeting, 1984

Welcome to you our distinguished guests.
You know we think you are the very best.

Yesterday as you toured our facility
I'm sure you could readily see
The people in Memphis are one big team
Adding value to the total Kellogg scene.

Commitment to growth is the slogan this year
So I say to you right now and here
The goal in Memphis is to grow the most
By urging all to serve Kellogg cereal instead of toast.

As we strive for a better way of life
We reach for opportunity and take hold
As we answer the challenge oh so bold
And promise to be committed to growth
from the depth of our being
But you say … seeing is believing.

All through our land as people exclaim
Who is that striped man anyway?
With lots of pride
We say today
Just step aside
And hear others say
Who are those people in Memphis
And how do they grow?

Easy – in 1984
More and More, they will show!
They are great!

Written by: *Vada Caldwell*

Only One Spark

It only takes a spark to get a fire going!
The Memphis team is on its way to showing
Just what we can do.
Passing on the spirit, spark by spark.

In building a fire, kindling wood makes a spark and creates a
blaze. Our people work hand in hand to kindle the spark of
leadership and share the spirit in many ways!

Working the Kellogg Way,
We carry out the Annual Theme
Sharing the spirit day by day
Leadership supported by one great team.

Some of our people are leaders
And some are kindling wood.
Helping kindle the spirit of the Kellogg family
Makes me feel really good.

Many of our people are special kindling
One works very hard every year
Making sure of good food and fellowship for each of us here.
So for all of us, I would like to say thanks
For giving that extra spark.
Her name is Becky Clark.

Written by: Vada Caldwell

February 21, 1986

Kellogg Corporate Annual

Meeting Feb. 22, 1986

Holiday Inn - Olive Branch, MS

Memphis Retirees Association News

Vada Caldwell

Vice-President and Reporter of the Association

I stay busy with that which I enjoy and yet have time to be still and reflect upon God's blessings. I was employed by Kellogg's from March 1959 thru April 1990 where I served in a variety of clerical positions. I thank God for the privilege of working for the company and the joy of making new friends.

I enjoy traveling, writing poetry, working with ceramics, and painting wood crafts made by my husband Tommy, who is retired from American Airlines. One of our greatest blessings is the joy of spending time with our three children and eight grandchildren. Also Tommy and I do volunteer work and are in the American Airlines retiree group, where I serve as secretary. In addition, I am the communications coordinator and treasurer of my church. I am currently writing our church history which is both exciting and challenging.

We work together, play together and live each day to the fullest and are very thankful for the many blessings we receive each day.

We help plan and coordinate our retiree trips. Our Florida tour was a great success. We wish all of you could have been with us for this wonderful trip. It was tremendously enjoyed by all, and we had a great time. Many interesting things happened during the trip, so I wrote a poem trying to include all the incidents. Of course, only those who went on the trip will know 'WHO' the poem is talking about.

We enjoyed the Florida Retirees Picnic in Bradenton. There were 58 present from the Memphis Retirees. Thirty-four including our driver, traveled on the bus. Twenty-four traveled by other modes of transportation.

Our Memphis family from Battle Creek were Don Thomason, Bob and Judy Martin, Bob and Diane Baskin, Paul Kehoe and Dave Walbridge. It was a real pleasure for us to see and visit with them. Memphis people took away ten door prizes. We hope to plan more trips and enjoy more fellowship. We invite all retirees to join us.

Our Poem

With great expectations and filled with glee
in the pouring down rain we left Memphis, Tennessee.
We shouted, "Off to Florida we go."
For fun, fellowship, and friendships to grow.

It rained throughout the day
Yet for the times we left the bus
The rain would go away
As though God did this just for us.

Every day was filled with lots of fun
Together we all became one.
We lived together for seven days
Going everywhere on our bus.
We didn't fret, we didn't fuss
We just enjoyed the sun rays.

We talked, we laughed, we shared
We ate lots of food which had been prepared
Everyone said try some of this and I'll eat some of that
Bite by bite to our bodies we added a little fat.

As he drove us day by day with zeal
Our driver held his hands steady on the wheel
We traveled together on the bus
And he joined right in as one of us
His name was Yater Shinall
He was loved and appreciated by all.

Oh the things day by day we learned.
She as a lady of fashion so pretty and fair

An earring of gold hung from one ear
And then as her head turned,
One of bright blue was shining there.
For one that forgets to pack toothpaste there is no hope,
It's like when you were naughty and had to wash
your mouth out with soap.

Driver, driver stop here please
I can hop that fence with the greatest of ease
I want to pick oranges from a tree
I will get one for you and one for me.
No, no, if caught you would pay a big fine
And in jail you would spend time.

What am I going to do?
I have lost my teeth, you see.
Let me look for you,
I'll help you find them she said
Maybe you lost them in bed,
Ouch, here they are, they just bit me!

Why is it when you grow old you begin to snore?
I know I never did do that before.
No, you just huffed in my ear
With a jab in the ribs I'd say, "Turn over dear."
Now I just tell you to turn over and face the wall
Or get up and go sleep in the hall.
He said, I know I used to huff instead of snore
Why don't you talk about oranges
And not talk about me anymore.

He reached in the cooler for a drink
Brakes were applied and before he could think
He fell into her lap
She did not retaliate with a slap
There was laughter and ballyhoo
And what a picture they made, those two.

Feel this side of my face
It's smooth and of whiskers there is no trace.
But now feel the other side
Here all the whiskers I cannot hide.
As I began to shave this morning a knock was heard at the door,
The bus is loading, are you ready to go?
She said, my goodness you are so slow,
Throw that razor in the bag and let's get on the bus
Before they go off and leave us.

We went to a dinner theatre called Arabian Nights,
Where we were entertained by the most beautiful sights.
While eating a delicious meal we were entranced
As the beautiful horses danced and pranced.
The performers and horses were elegantly dressed,
And by their daring feats we were impressed.

He said, I like the way I feel
There is nothing quite like good food
And the company of friends
To put you in a good mood.

He said, "Just three more days of vacation,
And we have to go back to retirement.

On this trip we really had a ball
And hope to take another sometime in the Fall.
Take us safely home now Dear Lord.
We will give You all the Glory, honor and Praise.
Throughout all the remainder of our days.

Written by: Vada Caldwell
Written about the Memphis Retirees' bus trip to Florida for
Kellogg retirees picnic in Bradenton.

Unleash the Power

1987 was a magic year
For which we give a great cheer.
Unleash the Power – Is the message of the hour.
The things we have seen and heard tonight
Assures us our future will be bright.
We can readily see – our unbeatable team is the key.
With pride, we join our special guests
In making our team the very best.

Written by:

Vada Caldwell

1988

1988 Corporate Communications Meeting
Friday, March 4, 1988 – Peabody Hotel

So Many Memories

It would take a book to share all our memories of the days we spent together. Our days of working together were filled with days of sharing both our joys and sorrows. And oh the joy of friends made over the years who still remain in our hearts.

After retirement, we enjoyed many trips together. We stayed in some really great places and some strange and you might even say some weird. Like the time we stopped late in the afternoon. We had to take our luggage to our rooms which was ok I guess. But would you believe our fellow traveler Horace Coleman had to call the desk and report his commode was not working and needed to be fixed. He was told they would take care of it right away. Almost immediately he heard a knock at his door and thought boy this is really service. He opened the door and was greeted by a young man who stated, "Here, I have a plunger for you". We all had a good laugh over such excellent service.

We could share lots more, but suffice it to say we had times of great joy on the trips and many, many memories of binding friendships made which still stand.

Written by:

Vada Caldwell

Retirement

I retired from Kellogg Company on April 30, 1990. I wrote an article for the New News magazine in 1991 and want to share it.

Retirement is a new way of life, but one of great joy, although I miss my friends and co-workers who were such an important part of my life for so many years. It seems impossible that as of April 30th I will have been retired one full year. A year filled to the brim with contentment. Each day is a new adventure. An adventure of finding that a happy life can be one filled with activity, or with quiet and relaxation. One filled with simple every day chores that bring a true sense of satisfaction and accomplishment. Seeing the world around us through the eyes of my grandchildren as we walk together in the woods and discover a tree with an unusual shape, a lizard, a bug, a special rock or a patch of wildflowers with their intricate beauty. As my grandson Russell puts it, "Mamaw, let's go discovering."

My hobby is working with ceramics. I read, write poetry, do volunteer work and stay busy enough to continue to grow. My husband, Tommy and I do volunteer work together and we travel.

My life is made even happier and more complete in the privilege of greeting the dawning of each new day with a thankful heart for all of God's blessings.

Ask me if I enjoy retirement and the resounding answer is "Yes, I recommend it highly." I would enjoy hearing from my friends and members of my Kellogg family.

Vada Caldwell

1991

Kellogg's Is People

Many years ago Will Keith Kellogg wrote:
"KELLOGG'S IS PEOPLE".

We these people have become a family of friends. We care about one another. We are always there to reach out with a helping hand when needed. We love and appreciate one another. I am blessed to have known each one of you.

With gladness of heart I remember our times together and am thankful for the privilege of calling you Friend!

May God bless each of us day by day and moment by moment as we travel the road of life before us.

With love and appreciation,

Vada Caldwell

2016

CPSIA information can be obtained
at www.ICGtesting.com
Printed in the USA
LVOW02*0756240317
528273LV00002B/2/P